Sound Activities

Extension Exercises

by Louise Lipscombe

Egon Publishers Ltd
618 Leeds Road, Outwood
Wakefield WF1 2LT
www.egon.co.uk

Sound Activities
Extension Exercises

Louise Lipscombe

ISBN: 978 1904160 62 5

Published in UK: 2002
Digital version: 2016

Egon Publishers Ltd
618 Leeds Road
Outwood
Wakefield WF1 2LT
Tel/FAX: 01924 871697
www.egon.co.uk
Company No: 1336483

Contents

Each of the units consists of three activity sheets,
listed as a, b, and c,

Order of Sounds

Introduction

These activity sheets have been devised to provide a useful resource to help and encourage children in developing phonic skills. They are aimed particularly at the child who has difficulty in retaining sounds, who may have poor short-term memory and would benefit from repetition and reinforcement. They may, however, be used by children of different ability levels and have already been in use for a number of years at Breakspear Junior School, in the London Borough of Hillingdon, where they have proved to be successful in providing the child with a more secure knowledge and understanding of phonics.

Each activity is designed to offer a different, challenging and enjoyable way of reinforcing spellings and word usage, helping children to become more confident with sounds and how they link into word families. There are four different activity sheets for each sound which are:

    a. Wordsearch
    b. Crossword
    c. Mixed Bag

a. Wordsearch

This activity is to encourage and reinforce:

- Sound and whole word recognition
- Tracking skills
- Skimming and scanning skills

It is suggested that once the word has been located it is underlined or circled,
then the **look-cover-write-check** strategy is used by writing the word on the line to the right.

b. Crossword

This activity is designed to encourage and reinforce:

- spatial awareness and organisation
- reading and comprehension skills
- extension of vocablary
- logical thinking -- existing letters can be used to help solve other clues
- self-correction -- the number of squares indicates how many letters are required

Answers are provided in a random order at the bottom of the sheet.

c. Mixed bag

This consists of a variety of stimulating exercises. These include: synonyms and atonyms, idioms, prefixes and suffixes, general knowledge questions, word games and more - designed to encourage and reinforce:

- dictionary skills
- spelling strategies
- an interest in words and their meaning
- use of a variety of reference books

It is suggested that students are instructed not to use a search engine or the internet in order that they discover alternative sources of information.

Louise Lipscombe

Name.............................. Date................................

Wordsearch

ar (air)

```
n  e  g  a  r  i  s  v  s  e  a  f  a  r  e  r  t
e  v  r  q  h  i  l  a  r  i  o  u  s  e  m  a  r
c  a  e  u  a  s  p  r  e  c  a  r  i  o  u  s  a
e  r  g  a  r  a  l  i  b  r  a  r  i  a  n  c  c
s  i  a  r  c  s  p  a  r  i  n  g  l  y  o  n  a
s  o  r  i  e  c  a  t  o  a  w  a  r  i  t  o  r
a  u  i  u  k  a  r  i  n  v  a  r  i  a  b  l  y
r  s  o  m  a  r  i  o  r  a  r  i  t  y  a  h  m
i  p  u  a  r  y  s  n  c  a  y  s  c  a  r  c  e
l  l  s  c  o  n  t  r  a  r  y  h  a  r  q  u  a
y  a  q  u  a  m  o  m  e  n  t  a  r  i  l  y  r
```

Find each hidden word and write it on the line provided.
Use the LOOK, SAY, COVER, WRITE, CHECK method.

aquarium	_____	precarious	_____
contrary	_____	rarity	_____
garish	_____	scarce	_____
gregarious	_____	scary	_____
hilarious	_____	seafarer	_____
invariably	_____	sparingly	_____
librarian	_____	variation	_____
momentarily	_____	various	_____
necessarily	_____	wary	_____

Name.............................. Date...................................

Crossword

ar (air)

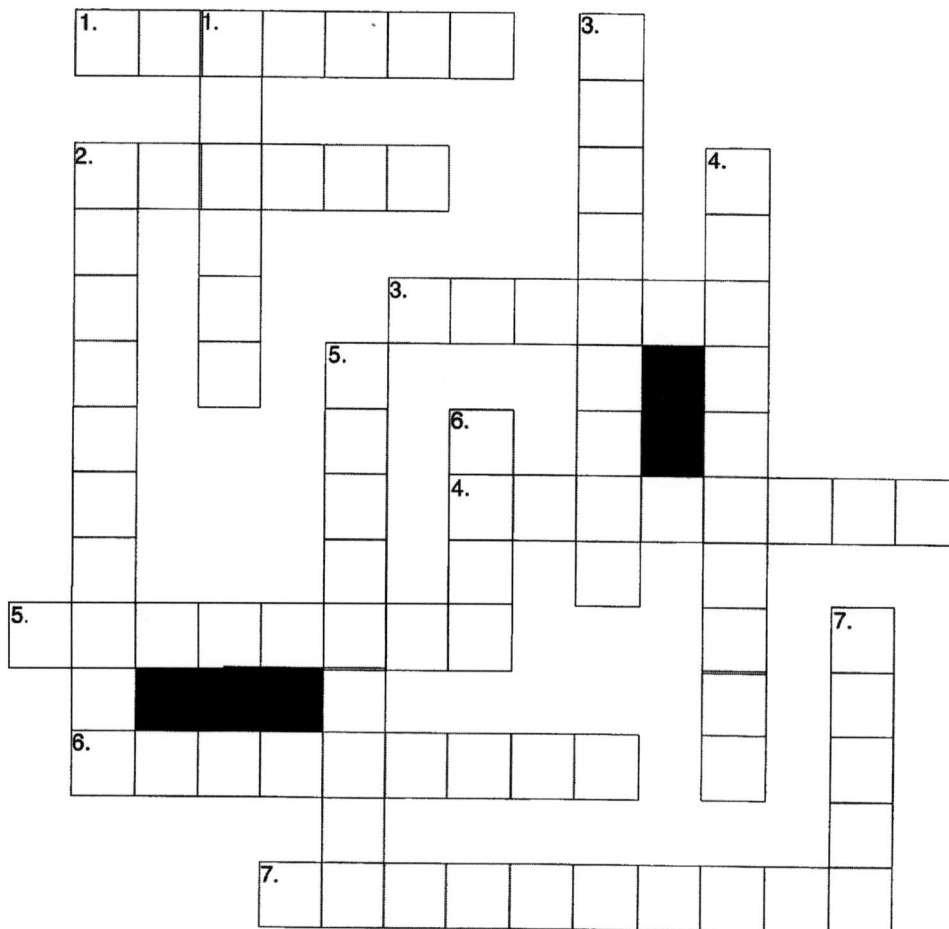

Across:

1. Different kinds.

2. Extremely bright and overdecorated.

3. In very short supply.

4. A large tank for fish.

5. Opposite or against.

6. Economically.

7. Always: without change.

Down:

1. An uncommon thing.

2. Likes being with others.

3. Extremely funny.

4. Risky; uncertain.

5. Someone who looks after a library.

6. Cautious; watchful.

7. Frightening.

scarce   hilarious   sparingly   precarious   scary   aquarium   garish
contrary   rarity   librarian   invariably   various   wary   gregarious

Name............................. Date....................................

Mixed Bag   ar (air)

Antonyms

Pair up the words which have opposite meanings. If you are not sure, use your dictionary to help you.

scarce   safe   abundance   variable   plentiful   gregarious   wary   lavish
constant   scarcity quiet   solitary   trusting   sparing   garish   precarious

1. _____ _____   5. _____ _____

2. _____ _____   6. _____ _____

3. _____ _____   7. _____ _____

4. _____ _____   8. _____ _____

Some General Knowledge Questions

Underline the word containing 'ar' (making the sound 'air') before answering the question. Use an encyclopedia, dictionary or atlas to help you, if you are not sure of the answer.

1.   Which insect spreads the disease called malaria? _____

2.   Which Egyptian pharaoh's tomb was discovered by Howard Carter in 1922?

     _____

3.   Name the royal father of Mary Tudor. _____

4.   Which animal is the symbol for the zodiac sign of Aries? _____

5.   How old is a centenarian? _____

6.   What particular food doesn't a vegetarian eat? _____

7.   What is a solarium? _____

8.   The Canary Islands are in the Atlantic Ocean, north-west of which continent?

     _____

9.   In which continent is the country of Hungary?_____

10. What is the capital city of Hungary? _____

11. Which English seafaring captain reached Australia in 1770? _____

12. 'Aquarium' comes from the Latin word 'aquarius '. What does 'aquarius' mean?

     _____

Odd One Out

Which of these is the odd one out and why?

    Libra   Capricorn   Gemini   Aquarium   Aries   Leo

_____

Wordsearch

ear (er)

```
a  p  h  r  o  s  m  i  s  h  e  a  r  d  i  s
r  e  s  e  a  r  c  h  j  e  a  r  m  l  e  e
e  a  r  h  t  a  r  e  h  e  r  g  s  k  a  a
h  r  y  e  a  s  r  b  e  w  o  r  e  a  r  r
e  l  e  a  r  n  e  d  a  r  v  e  a  r  k  c
a  t  a  r  e  h  e  a  r  s  e  a  r  l  y  h
r  u  r  s  k  e  a  r  s  h  r  o  c  i  v  l
n  e  n  a  e  a  r  c  e  u  h  e  h  s  e  i
e  a  r  l  a  m  t  w  e  m  e  a  r  t  a  g
s  r  e  a  r  t  h  e  n  w  a  r  e  n  r  h
t  p  a  e  a  r  u  n  e  a  r  t  h  e  t  t
e  a  r  t  h  q  u  a  k  e  d  c  h  e  a  r
```

Find each hidden word and write it on the line provided.
Use the LOOK, SAY, COVER, WRITE, CHECK method.

earl	_____	overheard	_____
early	_____	pearl	_____
earnest	_____	rehearsal	_____
earth	_____	rehearse	_____
earthenware	_____	research	_____
earthquake	_____	search	_____
hearse	_____	searchlight	_____
learned	_____	unearth	_____
misheard	_____	yearn	_____

Name........................... Date.................................

Crossword

ear (er)

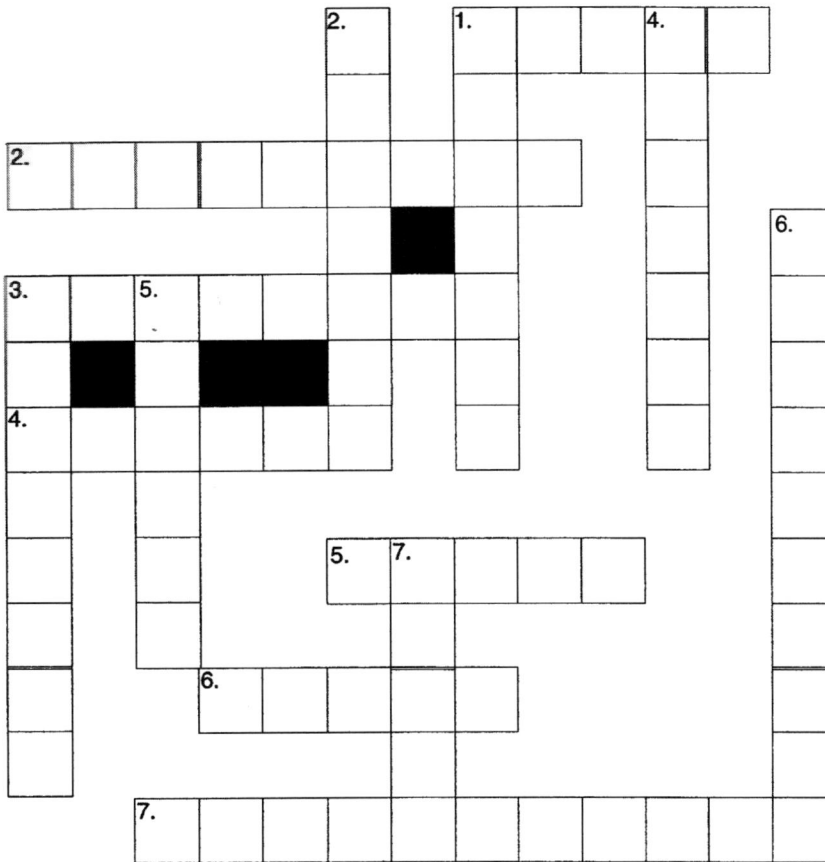

Across:

1. Opposite of late.

2. Past tense of overhear.

3. To practise for a performance.

4. To look for; to hunt for.

5. To long for something.

6. A small white ball formed in an oyster's shell and used in jewellery.

7. Pots and dishes made of baked clay.

Down:

1. Serious; determined.

2. To find by searching; to dig up.

3. A careful study to find out facts about something.

4. Having great knowledge which has been gained by studying.

5. A car used to carry a coffin at a funeral.

6. A violent shaking of the ground.

7. Our planet.

| rehearse | pearl | research | early | earthquake | yearn | Earth |
| learned | overheard | search | unearth | earthenware | hearse | earnest |

Name.............................. Date...................................

Mixed Bag ear (er)
Words Within Words

Solve the clue and write the word from the following list which has the answer inside it. The first one has been done for you.

early   earth   pearl   hearse   misheard   search   yearn   research
learned   earthenware   ~~rehearse~~   unearth   earnest

1.   take in sound through your ears   r e h e a r s e
2.   painting, drawing and sculpture   _ _ _ _ _
3.   opposite of far   _ _ _ _ _ _ _
4.   365 days   _ _ _ _ _
5.   a female chicken   _ _ _ _ _ _ _ _ _ _
6.   where a bird lays its   _ _ _ _ _ _ _
7.   a curved structure   _ _ _ _ _ _ _
8.   organs used for hear   _ _ _ _ _ _
9.   a fruit   _ _ _ _ _
10.   a nobleman   _ _ _ _
11.   to clip wool off a she   _ _ _ _ _ _ _
12.   salty water covering   _ _ _ _ _ _

Synonyms

Pair up the words which have similar meanings. If you are not sure, use your dictionary or thesaurus to help you.

earthenware   research   educated   hunt   rehearse   pottery   earth
long   investigate   unearth   sincere   premature   search   soil
early   practise   learned   yearn   discover   earnest

1. _____   _____   6. _____   _____
2. _____   _____   7. _____   _____
3. _____   _____   8. _____   _____
4. _____   _____   9. _____   _____
5. _____   _____   10. _____   _____

Find the Words

Looking for words inside a word can often help you to remember the spelling of a word. For example: words inside 'yearn' are 'year', 'ear' and 'earn'.
Can you find 10 words inside 'earthenware'?

_____   _____   _____   _____   _____

_____   _____   _____   _____   _____

A Proverb
What does 'the early bird catches the worm' mean?

_____

Wordsearch

o (ŭ)

```
e  d  i  s  c  o  v  e  r  f  o  v  e  w  a  c
a  i  d  o  m  e  r  e  c  o  v  e  r  o  n  t
c  s  i  m  o  n  g  r  e  l  c  l  o  n  i  o
c  c  s  e  s  h  o  v  e  l  o  m  e  d  w  n
o  o  c  t  o  v  e  n  t  o  n  g  u  e  e  g
m  l  o  i  w  o  w  o  m  e  f  u  o  r  l  e
p  o  m  m  o  c  o  n  j  u  r  e  m  f  c  w
a  u  f  e  n  o  v  e  r  c  o  m  e  u  o  o
n  r  o  s  t  o  m  a  c  h  n  e  a  l  m  n
y  f  r  o  c  o  m  f  o  r  t  a  b  l  e  d
d  e  t  a  c  c  o  m  p  l  i  s  h  o  v  e
```

Find each hidden word and write it on the line provided.
Use the LOOK, SAY, COVER, WRITE, CHECK method.

accompany	_____	overcome	_____
accomplish	_____	recover	_____
comfortable	_____	shove	_____
confront	_____	shovel	_____
conjure	_____	sometimes	_____
discolour	_____	stomach	_____
discomfort	_____	tongue	_____
discover	_____	welcome	_____
mongrel	_____	wonderful	_____

Name................................ Date....................................

Crossword

o (ŭ)

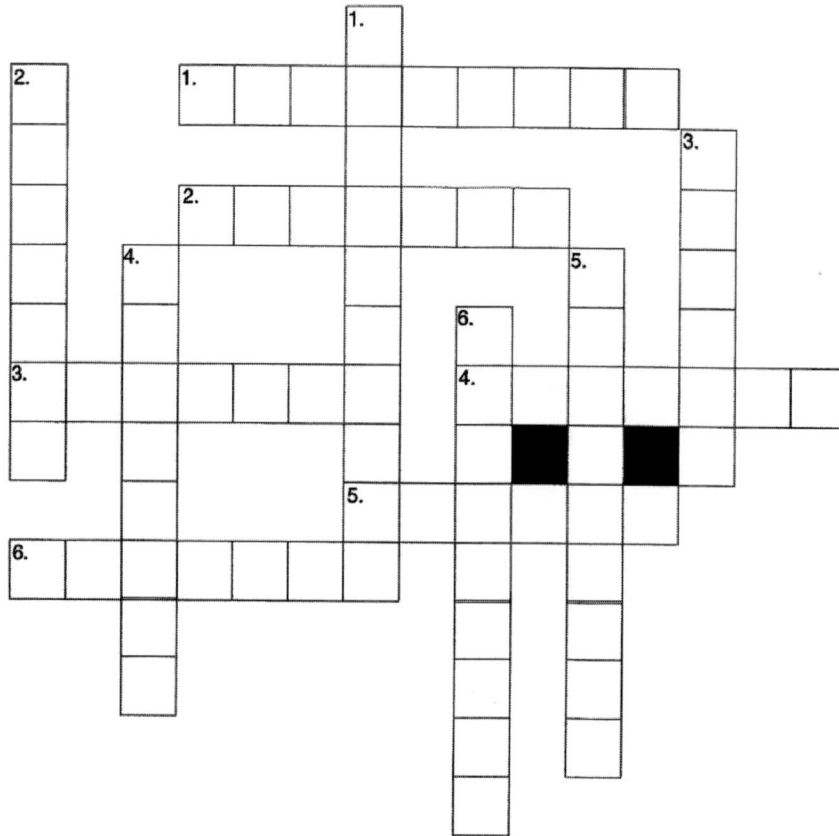

Across:

1. To spoil the colour of; to stain.

2. To get better after being ill.

3. A dog of mixed breeds.

4. To perform magic tricks.

5. A tool, similar to a spade.

6. An organ of the body which receives and digests food.

Down:

1. To do something successfully.

2. To greet with pleasure.

3. The organ in the mouth used for tasting, swallowing and speaking.

4. To face up to or oppose someone.

5. Marvellous.

6. To go somewhere with someone.

| conjure | confront | welcome | discolour | accompany | tongue |
| wonderful | recover | accomplish | stomach | shovel | mongrel |

| conjure | confront | welcome | discolour | accompany | tongue |
| wonderful | recover | accomplish | stomach | shovel | mongrel |

Name............................. Date...................................

Mixed Bag   o (ŭ)

Some General Knowledge Questions

Underline the word in the question which has the letter 'o' (making the short vowel sound 'u')
before answering it. If you are not sure of an answer, use a dictionary, encyclopedia or atlas to
help you.

1.   What do you call the place where monks live?   m o n _ _ _ _ _ _

2.   A coven is a collective noun for what type of people?   w _ _ _ _ _ _ _

3.   What colour is scarlet?   _____

4.   How many makes a 'baker's dozen'?   _____

5.   What is the job of the stomach in the body?   _____

      _____

6.   Name two counties which border the county of Somerset in the south-west of England.

      _____

7.   What acrobatic movement would you be doing if you performed a somersault?

      _____

8.   How does Monday get its name?   _____

Idioms
Money, Money, Money!

These expressions all have money in them. Match the expression with its meaning. The first
one has been done for you.

Idiom	Meaning
to have money to burn	people with a lot of money have power and influence to get what they want.
money for old rope	to have so much money that it doesn't matter if it's wasted.
to spend money like water	to spend a lot of money in an attempt to regain money already lost.
money talks	to spend a lot of money unnecessarily.
to throw good money after bad	money earned for little or no effort.

Words Within the Word

Without changing the position of the letters, how many words can you find inside 'comfortable'?
Write them here.

_____

_____

Sound Activities - Extension Exercises

Wordsearch

Silent t

s	t	r	u	s	t	l	e	t	g	m	o	r	s	t	a
m	r	a	s	b	e	i	r	a	r	o	r	t	o	m	p
o	n	p	r	u	s	s	c	l	i	r	s	m	f	o	c
i	o	p	p	s	t	t	h	i	s	t	l	e	t	r	u
s	j	o	s	t	l	e	r	i	t	g	t	s	e	t	s
t	e	r	t	l	e	n	e	s	l	i	e	t	n	g	t
e	s	t	l	e	m	e	s	n	e	s	t	l	e	a	l
n	a	p	p	o	b	r	i	s	t	l	e	e	r	g	e
m	i	s	t	l	e	t	o	e	g	l	i	s	t	e	n

Find each hidden word and write it on the line provided.
Use the LOOK, SAY, COVER, WRITE, CHECK method.

bristle	_____	moisten	_____
bustle	_____	mortgage	_____
glisten	_____	nestle	_____
gristle	_____	rapport	_____
jostle	_____	rustle	_____
listener	_____	softener	_____
mistletoe	_____	thistle	_____

Name.............................. Date...................................

Crossword

Silent t

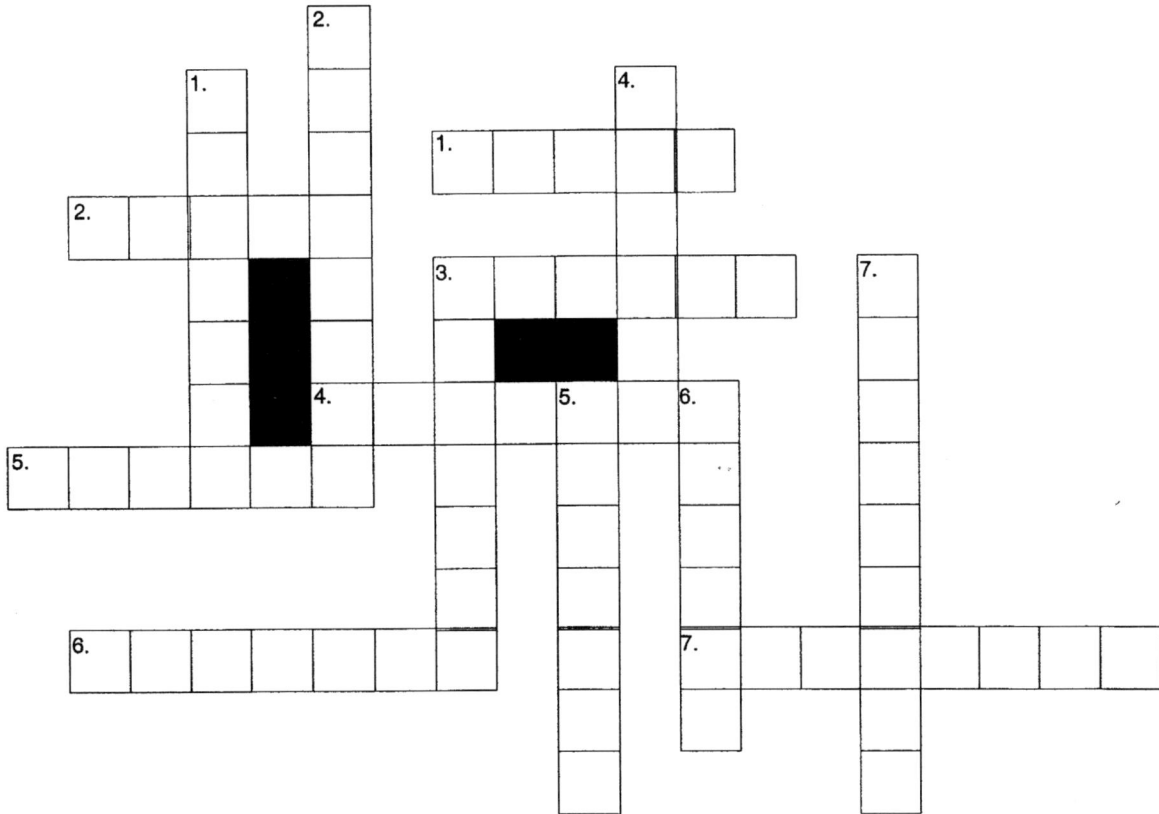

Across:

1. A performer's first appearance in public.

2. A garage for buses or lorries.

3. To rush about busily.

4. To shine like something that is wet.

5. To push someone roughly.

6. The tough, rubbery substance in meat; cartilage.

7. A person who tunes in to a radio programme.

Down:

1. A feeling of understanding between people.

2. An agreement for borrowing money to buy a house.

3. A stiff, coarse hair.

4. The sound of leaves blowing in the wind.

5. A wild plant with prickly leaves and purple flowers.

6. To lie or sit closely together.

7. A plant with white berries, which grows on some trees.

| mistletoe | mortgage | glisten | listener | jostle | nestle | rapport |
| debut | bustle | depot | gristle | bristle | thistle | rustle |

Mixed Bag

Silent t

Anagrams

Rearrange the letters of these anagrams to make the following words.

BUSTLE	GRISTLE	MORTGAGE	RUSTLE	SOFTENER	RAPPORT
	BRISTLE	JOSTLE	THISTLE	MISTLETOE	

1. ART PROP _____
2. GREAT MOG _____
3. HE TILTS _____
4. BLISTER _____
5. RESULT _____

6. BLUEST _____
7. ST JOEL _____
8. MOST ELITE _____
9. STERN FOE _____
10. STIR GEL _____

IDIOMS

What is meant by each of these expressions?

1. to wet one's whistle
   - to blow the whistle at the end of a football match.
   - to drop a whistle in a puddle.
   - to have a drink.

2. to rustle up something
   - to perform a magic trick.
   - to make something quickly.
   - to move in the wind.

3. to build castles in the air
   - to build on top of a high hill.
   - to be good at building sandcastles.
   - to have unrealistic plans for the future.

Words Within Words

Solve the clue and write the word from the following list which has the answer inside it. The first one has been done for you.

mistletoe ~~bustle~~ depot debut rapport rustle

1. a form of transport b u s t l e
2. a pan _ _ _ _ _ _
3. a fog _ _ _ _ _ _ _ _ _
4. corrosion formed on iron _ _ _ _ _ _
5. a connective in a sentence _ _ _ _ _
6. where goods pass in and out of a country by sea or air _ _ _ _ _ _ _

Sound Activities - Extension Exercises

Name............................. Date..................................

Wordsearch

```
n  d  e  s  i  n  c  e  r  e  d  s  e  i  e  a
a  e  r  e  h  t  h  x  e  x  u  p  k  n  u  s
c  l  o  v  p  h  a  c  a  t  h  l  e  t  e  t
o  e  s  e  r  e  n  e  s  r  l  e  b  e  m  a
m  t  c  r  a  m  i  n  t  e  r  f  e  r  e  m
p  e  h  e  l  e  v  e  h  m  t  e  s  v  x  p
e  r  e  c  e  d  e  b  e  e  a  d  h  e  r  e
t  e  m  a  t  m  o  s  p  h  e  r  e  n  u  d
e  g  e  f  e  s  e  p  e  r  s  e  v  e  r  e
n  c  o  m  p  l  e  t  e  s  u  p  r  e  m  e
```

Find each hidden word and write it on the line provided.
Use the LOOK, SAY, COVER, WRITE, CHECK method.

adhere	_____	persevere	_____
athlete	_____	recede	_____
atmosphere	_____	scheme	_____
compete	_____	serene	_____
complete	_____	severe	_____
delete	_____	sincere	_____
extreme	_____	stampede	_____
interfere	_____	supreme	_____
intervene	_____	theme	_____

Sound Activities - Extension Exercises

Crossword

e e

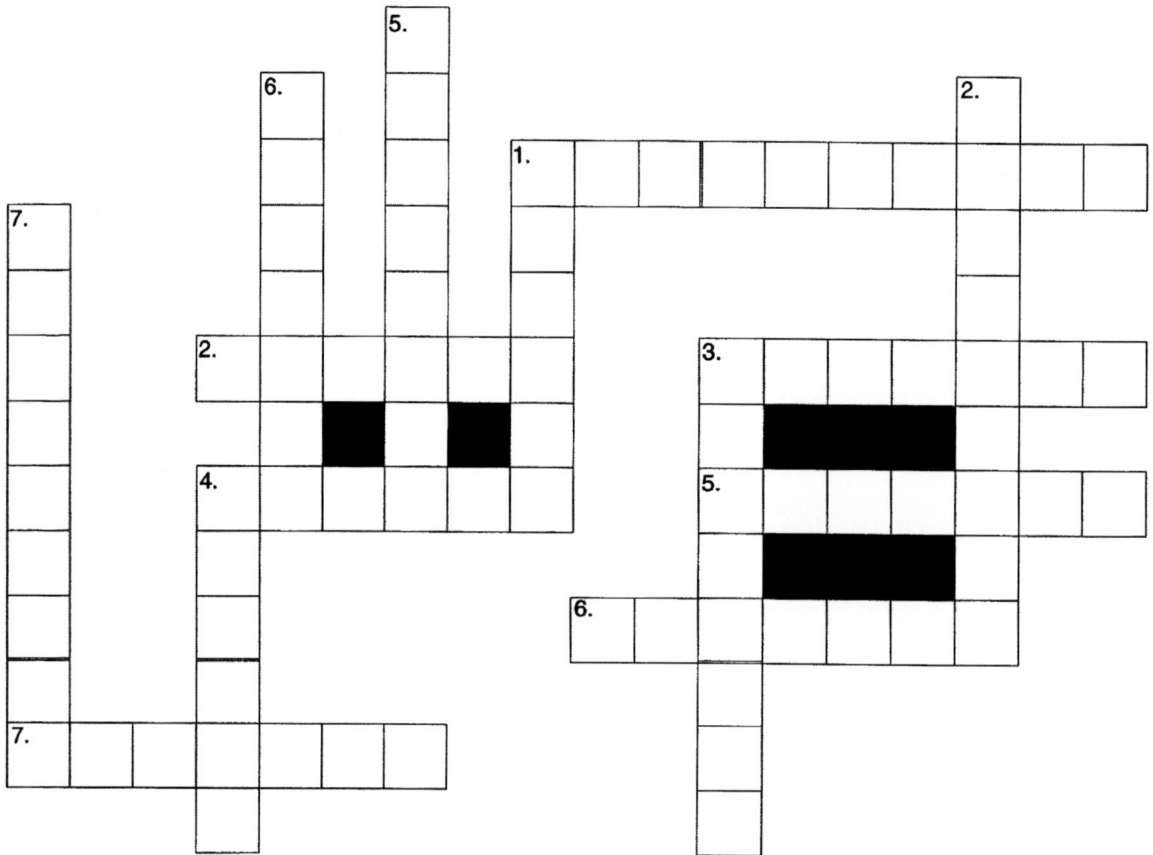

Across:

1. The air surrounding the Earth.

2. To shrink back or to go back.

3. Genuine; honest.

4. Peaceful and quiet.

5. A person who takes part in sports.

6. The most important; the highest or greatest.

7. Severe; very far away.

Down:

1. To stick.

2. To keep trying, regardless of how difficult something is to do.

3. Many animals or people suddenly rushing together.

4. Harsh.

5. To finish.

6. To take part in a challenge against someone else.

7. To come between.

| supreme | compete | intervene | sincere | stampede | severe | recede |
| persevere | atmosphere | complete | athlete | adhere | extreme | serene |

5b

Mixed Bag

Solve me - if you can!

My first is in athlete, but not in compete;   _____

My second is in recede and also in stampede;   _____

My third is in theme, but not in extreme;   _____

This is twice in scheme and thrice in intervene;   _____

There are two in interfere, but only one in sincere;   _____

My last is twice in complete and thrice in delete.   _____

Stick to what you are doing and you'll get it! The word is _____

Nouns and Adjectives

Sort the following nouns and adjectives in to the correct columns.
The first ones have been done for you.

serenity	athletic	supreme	extremity	sincere	severity
extreme	serene	sincerity	~~atmosphere~~	athlete	supremacy
severe	~~atmospheric~~				

Noun	Adjective
atmosphere	atmospheric

Countries and People

People from China are called Chinese. Which of the following countries have people ending in '-ese'? The first one has been done for you.

| France | ~~China~~ | Japan | Egypt | Vietnam | Portugal | Canada |
| Lebanon | Finland | Spain | Sudan | Italy | Mexico | Burma | Malta | Turkey |

Country	People
China	Chinese

Country	People

Name............................... Date....................................

Wordsearch

```
i  p  c  i  g  h  t  b  u  p  r  i  g  h  t  r  f  s
u  i  h  h  i  g  h  l  i  g  h  t  e  n  r  i  o  f
n  g  e  o  n  f  r  i  g  h  t  f  u  l  i  g  r  l
s  h  a  u  s  o  m  g  c  o  p  y  r  i  g  h  t  o
i  t  d  j  i  g  t  h  e  i  g  h  t  e  n  t  n  o
g  p  l  i  g  h  t  t  a  r  n  i  g  i  m  e  i  d
h  s  i  g  h  t  s  e  e  i  n  g  i  g  i  o  g  l
t  k  g  h  t  h  e  c  i  g  h  t  g  h  t  u  h  i
l  g  h  t  e  f  o  r  e  s  i  g  h  t  g  s  t  g
y  b  t  e  n  l  i  g  h  t  e  n  t  s  i  g  t  h
a  i  r  t  i  g  h  t  f  o  r  t  h  r  i  g  h  t
```

Find each hidden word and write it on the line provided.
Use the LOOK, SAY, COVER, WRITE, CHECK method.

airtight	_____	headlight	_____
blight	_____	heighten	_____
copyright	_____	highlight	_____
enlighten	_____	insight	_____
floodlight	_____	plight	_____
foresight	_____	righteous	_____
forthright	_____	sightseeing	_____
fortnight	_____	unsightly	_____
frightful	_____	upright	_____

Sound Activities - Extension Exercises

Name............................   Date....................................

Crossword   igh

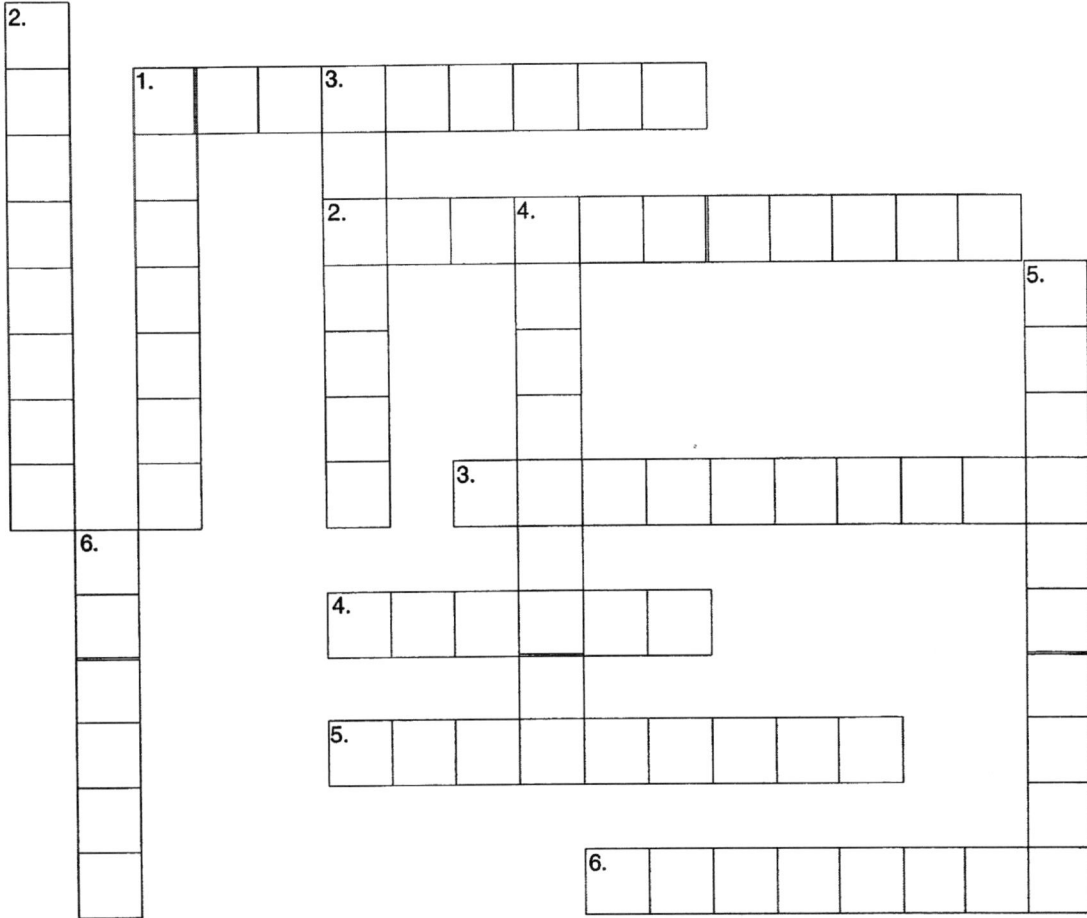

Across:

1. Not very pleasant to look at.

2. Visiting and looking at places of interest.

3. A lamp giving a wide, bright beam, especially outside.

4. A disease of a plant.

5. A period of two weeks.

6. Sealed, not letting air get in or out.

Down:

1. Vertical.

2. To make something higher or to make a feeling more intense.

3. An understanding of something.

4. The most interesting and exciting part of something.

5. Outspoken; frank.

6. A difficult or distressing situation.

| fortnight | insight | airtight | sightseeing | blight | heighten |
| floodlight | highlight | unsightly | forthright | plight | upright |

Sound Activities - Extension Exercises

Mixed Bag

igh

Homophones

Homophones are words which sound the same, but are spelt differently - from the Greek words 'homos' meaning 'same' and 'phone' meaning 'sound'. Write down homophones of these words.

1. side _____
2. write _____
3. night _____
4. incite _____
5. Titan _____

6. might _____
7. higher _____
8. size _____
9. sight _____
10. sleight _____

What is the difference in meaning between 'lightning' and lightening'?

lightning : _____

lightening : _____

Similes

Can you complete these similes using words with 'igh' in them?

1. as quick as _____

2. as_____ as a feather

3. as _____ as rain

4. as _____ as a drum

Idioms

Match each expression with its meaning.

Idiom	Meaning
to keep a tight rein on something	to spend less money and be careful with it
in a tight corner	to be the centre of public attention
to tighten one's belt	the kind of thing you like to know about
for the high jump	to be in a difficult situation
as right as rain	to pay far too much for something
right up your street	about to be severely punished
in the limelight	to keep something under control
highway robbery	feeling fit and healthy

Wordsearch

are (air)

```
d  e  s  t  a  r  e  g  a  r  e  s  t  r  o  c
f  x  t  h  o  c  h  l  i  c  s  q  u  a  n  r
a  p  o  r  m  a  t  a  s  o  p  u  a  b  i  u
r  a  r  e  q  u  a  r  e  m  u  a  r  e  g  b
e  l  w  a  s  a  r  e  k  p  a  r  b  v  h  a
w  a  e  d  n  i  b  e  w  a  r  e  n  a  t  r
e  r  l  b  a  r  e  l  y  r  e  l  a  r  m  e
l  e  f  a  r  n  s  p  r  e  p  a  r  e  a  f
l  d  a  r  e  d  e  v  i  l  a  m  e  a  r  o
w  a  r  e  h  o  u  s  e  t  o  f  a  r  e  o
s  h  e  m  o  d  e  c  l  a  r  e  v  e  m  t
```

Find each hidden word and write it on the line provided.
Use the LOOK, SAY, COVER, WRITE, CHECK method.

barefoot	_____	nightmare	_____
barely	_____	prepare	_____
beware	_____	rare	_____
compare	_____	snare	_____
daredevil	_____	square	_____
declare	_____	stare	_____
fare	_____	threadbare	_____
farewell	_____	warehouse	_____
glare	_____	welfare	_____

Name............................ Date...............................

Crossword

are (air)

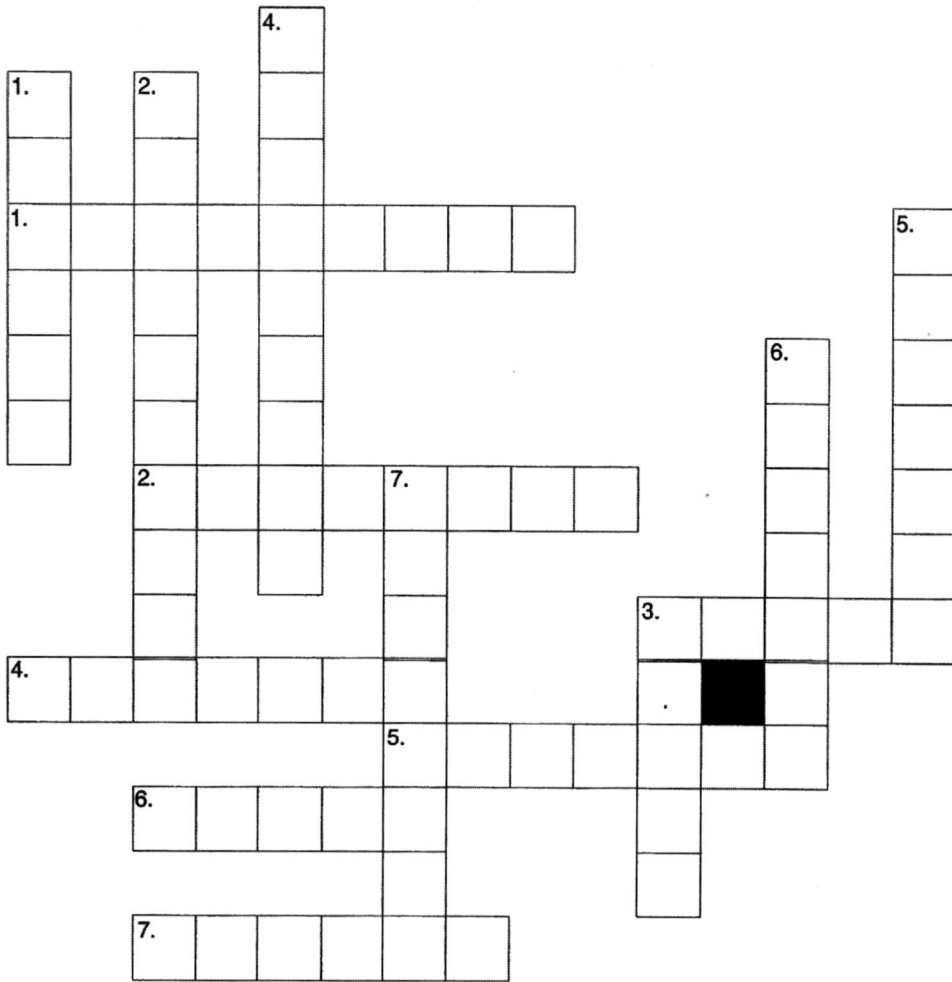

Across:

1. A large building used for storing goods.

2. Without shoes or socks on.

3. To look continuously at something with wide-open eyes.

4. To get ready or to make ready.

5. People's health and happiness.

6. A strong, dazzling light.

7. Scarcely; only just.

Down:

1. Be careful; be on your guard.

2. How fabric is when it is worn so that threads are showing.

3. A trap.

4. A very bad dream.

5. To announce or make known publicly.

6. To liken; to look for similarities.

7. Goodbye.

| stare | nightmare | welfare | barely | declare | warehouse | glare |
| prepare | threadbare | beware | compare | farewell | barefoot | snare |

7b

Name............................. Date................................

Mixed Bag   are (air)

Homophones

Homophones are words which sound the same, but are spelt differently - from the Greek words 'homos' meaning 'same' and 'phone' meaning 'sound'. Use your dictionary to find the different meanings of these homophones.

mare : _____

mayor : _____

flare : _____

flair : _____

fare : _____

fair : _____

compare : _____

compere : _____

pare : _____

pair : _____

pear : _____

hair : _____

hare : _____

Idioms

What is meant by each of these expressions?

1.   a square meal   - a meal served on a square plate.
                              - a balanced and nutritious meal.
                              - a sandwich.

2.   a square deal   - a fair and honest deal or bargain.
                              - people playing cards at a square table.
                              - a traditional dance.

3.   back to square one   - to lose at a board game.
                              - to start again at the beginning.
                              - a game of hopscotch.

A Cryptic Clue
Find the mystery word by solving the cryptic clue.

A female horse in the dark, maybe?   n _ _ _ _ _ _ _

Wordsearch cc (hard c / soft c)

```
e  m  b  r  a  c  c  e  p  t  s  u  c  c  e  s  s
s  s  u  c  c  e  s  t  i  b  l  u  a  c  c  e  u
u  t  a  c  c  e  p  t  a  b  l  e  c  h  o  k  c
c  r  c  e  e  c  g  e  c  c  w  b  c  c  v  l  c
c  a  c  c  s  c  w  a  c  c  e  l  e  r  a  t  e
e  c  e  c  s  t  a  j  i  h  n  o  s  a  c  e  s
s  c  n  f  o  j  c  o  d  a  k  i  s  c  c  r  s
s  i  t  u  r  e  c  c  e  n  t  r  i  c  i  v  i
f  n  p  c  y  a  w  p  n  t  a  c  c  o  n  i  o
u  v  a  c  c  i  n  a  t  e  d  i  l  b  e  n  n
l  j  e  g  e  v  a  c  c  e  n  t  u  a  t  e  n
```

Find each hidden word and write it on the line provided.
Use the LOOK, SAY, COVER, WRITE, CHECK method.

accelerate	_____	accident	_____
accent	_____	eccentric	_____
accentuate	_____	success	_____
accept	_____	successful	_____
acceptable	_____	succession	_____
access	_____	vaccinate	_____
accessory	_____	vaccine	_____

Name............................. Date...................................

Crossword

cc (hard c / soft c)

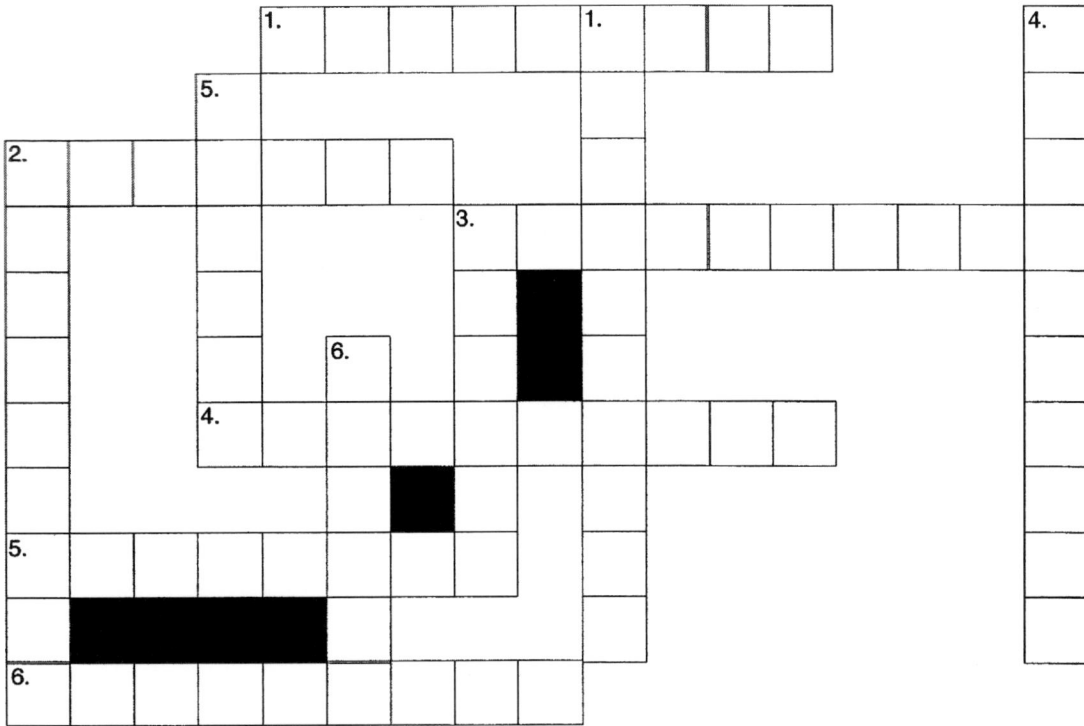

Across:

1. A person who assists in a crime.

2. A substance used for inoculation against disease.

3. To go faster.

4. Having success.

5. An event which was not meant to happen.

6. Odd or strange.

Down:

1. The process of following in order.

2. Inoculate to prevent disease.

3. The particular way words are pronounced locally or nationally.

4. To emphasise; to stress.

5. The way in to somewhere.

6. To take something offered to you.

successful   access   eccentric   vaccinate   accelerate   accept
accident   succession   vaccine   accent   accessory   accentuate

Mixed Bag

cc (hard c / soft c)

Verbs and Nouns

Complete the columns with either the verb or the noun. If you are not sure, use your dictionary to help you.

Verb	Noun
accelerate	
	acceptance
	success
accentuate	
	accession
vaccinate	

Confusing Words

Use your dictionary to find the difference in meaning between these pairs of words.

accept : _____

except : _____

access : _____

excess : _____

accent : _____

ascent : _____

accede : _____

exceed : _____

The Right Word

Circle the correct word from the brackets to complete the sentence.

1. He was pleased to (except, accept) the invitation to their wedding.

2. Kate was unable to (access, excess) the computer program without the password.

3. The old lady has a broad Scottish (ascent, accent).

4. It is most likely that the Queen's eldest son will (exceed, accede) to the throne.

8c

Name.............................. Date..................................

Wordsearch ph

```
p  a  t  a  t  p  h  e  m  i  s  p  h  e  r  e  f  p
h  t  y  p  a  m  p  h  l  e  t  h  p  h  o  m  p  h
a  m  p  h  e  p  h  a  p  h  o  a  h  g  a  p  h  a
d  o  h  a  g  r  a  p  h  i  c  s  i  m  p  h  o  t
o  s  o  n  r  o  s  p  h  e  r  i  c  a  l  a  t  y
l  p  n  t  e  p  e  d  o  l  p  h  a  c  e  s  o  p
p  h  s  o  p  h  i  s  t  i  c  a  t  e  d  i  g  h
h  e  t  m  h  i  o  p  h  e  r  e  b  o  r  s  e  o
i  r  a  l  p  h  a  b  e  t  i  c  a  l  a  p  n  o
n  e  p  h  o  t  o  c  o  p  i  e  r  a  p  h  i  n
a  d  e  c  i  p  h  e  r  m  p  r  o  p  h  e  c  y
```

Find each hidden word and write it on the line provided.
Use the LOOK, SAY, COVER, WRITE, CHECK method.

alphabetical	_____	phantom	_____
atmosphere	_____	phase	_____
decipher	_____	photocopier	_____
dolphin	_____	photogenic	_____
emphasis	_____	prophecy	_____
graphics	_____	sophisticated	_____
hemisphere	_____	spherical	_____
pamphlet	_____	typhoon	_____

Name............................... Date...................................

Crossword

ph

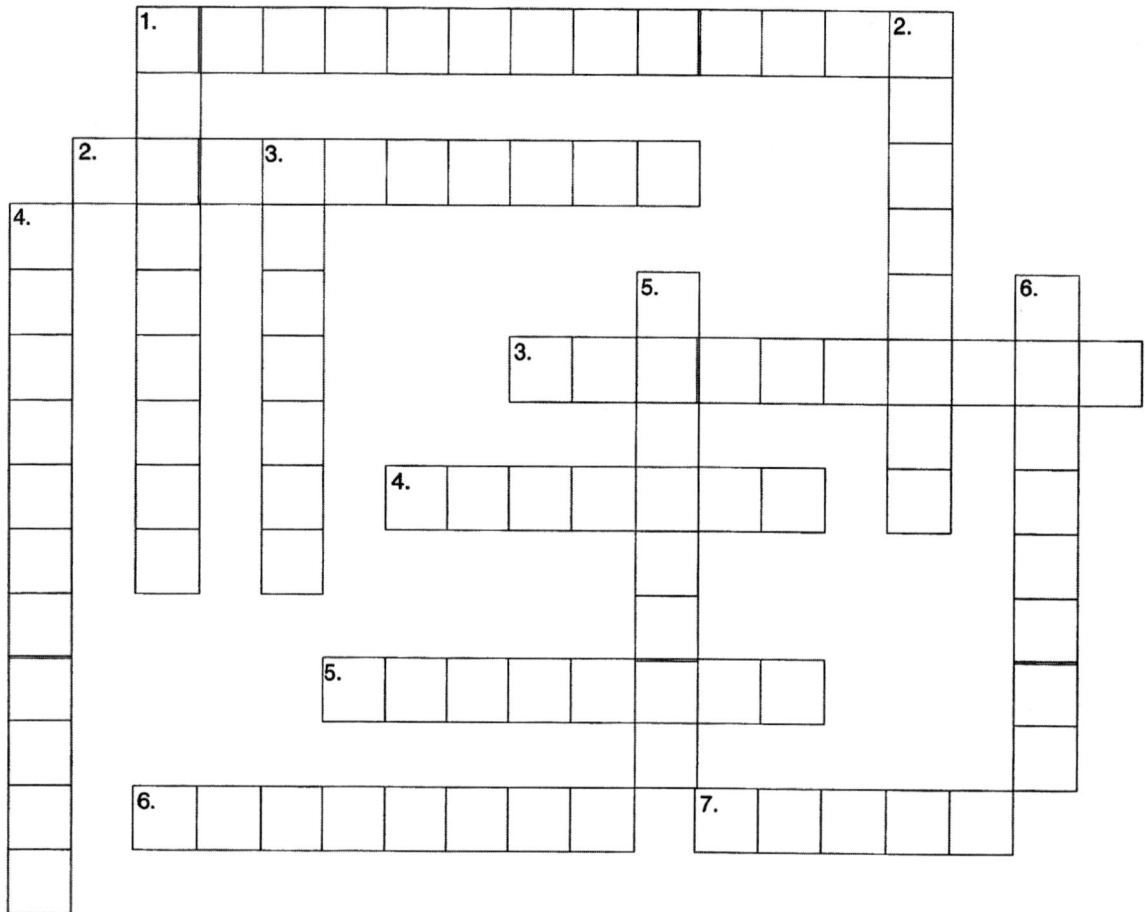

Across:

1. Highly developed and complex.

2. Having an appearance which looks very pleasing in photographs.

3. The gases surrounding a planet.

4. A sea mammal.

5. Pictures on a computer screen.

6. A small, unbound information leaflet.

7. Each stage of a plan.

Down:

1. In the shape of a ball.

2. To unravel a code so that it can be understood.

3. A violent, windy storm.

4. A machine which copies printed sheets of paper.

5. Special importance attached to something.

6. Something which someone says will happen in the future.

graphics   typhoon   phase   photocopier   prophecy   emphasis   dolphin
photogenic   spherical   atmosphere   pamphlet   sophisticated   decipher

9b

Sound Activities - Extension Exercises

Name............................. Date....................................

Mixed Bag ph

Phone Home!

You have been given the suffix '-phone'. Read the clues and write the answers using the correct prefixes from below.

mega-　　　xylo-　　　head-　　　tele-　　　saxo-

1. A device for communicating over long distances　　　_ _ _ _ phone

2. A brass wind instrument　　　_ _ _ _ phone

3. Worn on the head for listening to music　　　_ _ _ _ phones

4. A funnel-shaped device for making a person's voice louder　　　_ _ _ _ phone

5. A musical instrument made of wooden bars which are hit with small hammers　　　_ _ _ _ phone

The Suffix '-graph'

You have been given the suffix '-graph'. Read the clues and write the answers using the correct prefixes from below.

photo-　　　auto-　　　para-　　　tele-　　　seismo-

1. One or more sentences on one theme　　　_ _ _ _ _ graph

2. Taken with a camera　　　_ _ _ _ _ _ graph

3. Instrument for measuring earthquakes　　　_ _ _ _ _ _ _ graph

4. A person's signature　　　_ _ _ _ _ graph

5. A way of sending messages by using an electrical current　　　_ _ _ _ graph

The suffix '-graph' comes from the Greek language. Use an etymological dictionary (one which gives origins of words) to find out what it means. _____

'Graphy' Words

The answers to these clues end in '-graphy'. Do you know what they are?

1. A study of the earth, its climate, its people, etc.　　　_ _ _ graphy

2. Artistic handwriting　　　_ _ _ _ _ graphy

3. The story of someone's life　　　_ _ _ graphy

4. Taking pictures with a camera　　　_ _ _ _ _ graphy

5. The story of someone's life written by himself or herself.　　　_ _ _ _ _ _ _ graphy

Wordsearch

cc (hard c

```
o  b  l  a  c  c  l  a  i  m  u  s  s  k  p  a  s
c  o  a  c  c  o  m  p  a  n  y  o  u  r  c  c  p
c  c  e  c  o  c  c  u  p  y  o  c  c  u  r  c  a
a  c  c  u  r  a  t  e  n  t  a  c  c  l  s  l  c
s  u  i  m  p  e  c  c  a  b  l  e  u  c  u  i  c
i  p  l  u  e  a  c  c  o  n  a  r  l  c  c  m  o
o  a  m  l  c  i  m  p  e  c  c  b  e  l  c  a  m
n  t  a  a  c  c  o  u  n  t  c  r  n  a  u  t  p
e  i  t  t  u  c  d  c  e  p  r  i  t  i  m  i  l
n  o  d  e  s  i  c  c  a  t  e  c  e  n  b  z  i
t  n  a  c  c  o  m  m  o  d  a  t  i  o  n  e  c
a  c  c  o  m  p  l  i  s  h  a  c  c  u  p  y  e
```

Find each hidden word and write it on the line provided.
Use the LOOK, SAY, COVER, WRITE, CHECK method.

acclaim	_____	desiccate	_____
acclimatize	_____	impeccable	_____
accommodation	_____	occasion	_____
accompany	_____	occupation	_____
accomplice	_____	occupy	_____
accomplish	_____	occur	_____
account	_____	soccer	_____
accumulate	_____	succulent	_____
accurate	_____	succumb	_____

10a

Name.............................. Date....................................

Crossword

cc (hard c)

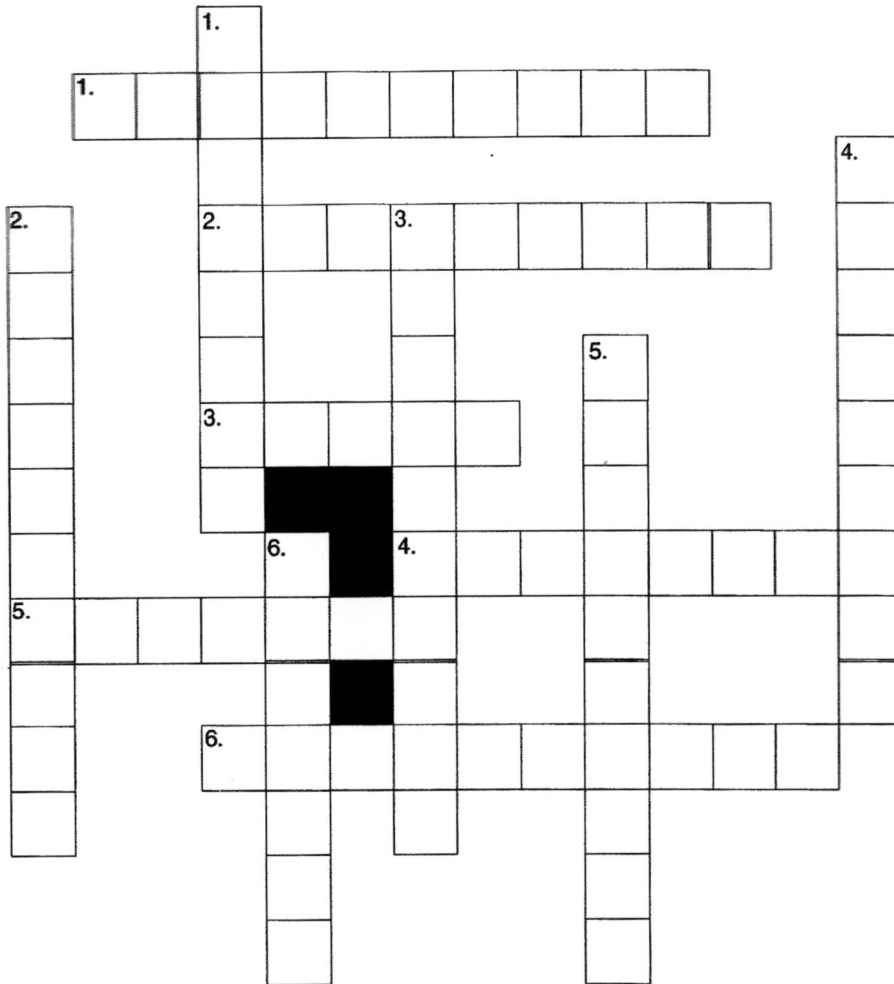

Across:

1. A partner in crime.

2. To go with someone.

3. To happen.

4. Correct in every detail.

5. An amount of money someone keeps in a bank.

6. To achieve.

Down:

1. A particular time when something happens.

2. Faultless.

3. Someone's job.

4. Juicy.

5. To gather or collect.

6. To be forced to give way to something.

occur   succulent   account   succumb   accompany   accurate
accumulate   impeccable   occasion   accomplish   accomplice   occupation

10b

Name............................... Date...................................

Mixed Bag cc (hard c)

Synonyms

From the words below, find 14 pairs which have similar meanings. If you are not sure, use your dictionary or thesaurus to help you.

occasion   accompany   exact   lodgings   accomplice   succulent
happen   event   occupation   occur   football   report   escort   familiar
accomplish   job   soccer   accurate   blame   accustomed   account
partner   juicy   accommodation   achieve   collect   accuse   accumulate

1. _____ _____   8. _____ _____

2. _____ _____   9. _____ _____

3. _____ _____   10. _____ _____

4. _____ _____   11. _____ _____

5. _____ _____   12. _____ _____

6. _____ _____   13. _____ _____

7. _____ _____   14. _____ _____

NOTE: the word 'soccer' has a hard 'c' sound even though 'c' is followed by 'e'.

Definitions

Use your dicitionary to find the meaning of each of these words.

desiccate : _____

_____

acclaim : _____

_____

acclimatize : _____

_____

Use your dictionary to find two meanings of 'account'. Write them here.

1. _____

2. _____

How Many Words Can You 'Accumulate'?

From the list below, find and write the words which have a similar meaning to 'accumulate'. If you are not sure, use your dictionary or thesaurus.

assemble   disperse   gather   accrue   dispose   collect
separate   amass   scatter   distribute   muster

_____

_____

10c

Sound Activities - Extension Exercises

Name............................. Date...................................

Wordsearch ui (oo)

```
g  r  o  f  u  i  b  t  r  u  i  t  f  u  i  s  k
r  i  r  r  p  u  r  s  u  i  t  r  r  l  m  u  o
a  r  u  u  i  j  u  i  s  t  r  a  u  f  s  i  c
p  e  i  f  n  u  i  s  a  n  c  e  i  r  p  t  r
e  c  t  r  u  i  s  u  b  e  r  u  t  u  a  c  u
f  r  j  u  i  c  e  i  o  b  u  i  y  i  c  a  i
r  u  s  i  c  y  i  t  j  u  i  c  o  t  e  s  s
u  i  p  t  e  b  r  u  h  i  s  t  u  f  s  e  e
i  t  r  e  c  r  u  i  t  m  e  n  t  u  u  f  r
t  s  l  u  i  c  e  u  l  u  i  c  e  l  i  t  c
a  n  u  i  c  y  s  u  i  t  a  b  l  e  t  r  t
```

Find each hidden word and write it on the line provided.
Use the LOOK, SAY, COVER, WRITE, CHECK method.

bruise	_____	nuisance	_____
cruise	_____	pursuit	_____
cruiser	_____	recruit	_____
fruit	_____	recruitment	_____
fruitful	_____	sluice	_____
fruity	_____	spacesuit	_____
grapefruit	_____	suit	_____
juice	_____	suitable	_____
juicy	_____	suitcase	_____

11a

Name............................ Date.................................

Crossword

ui (oo)

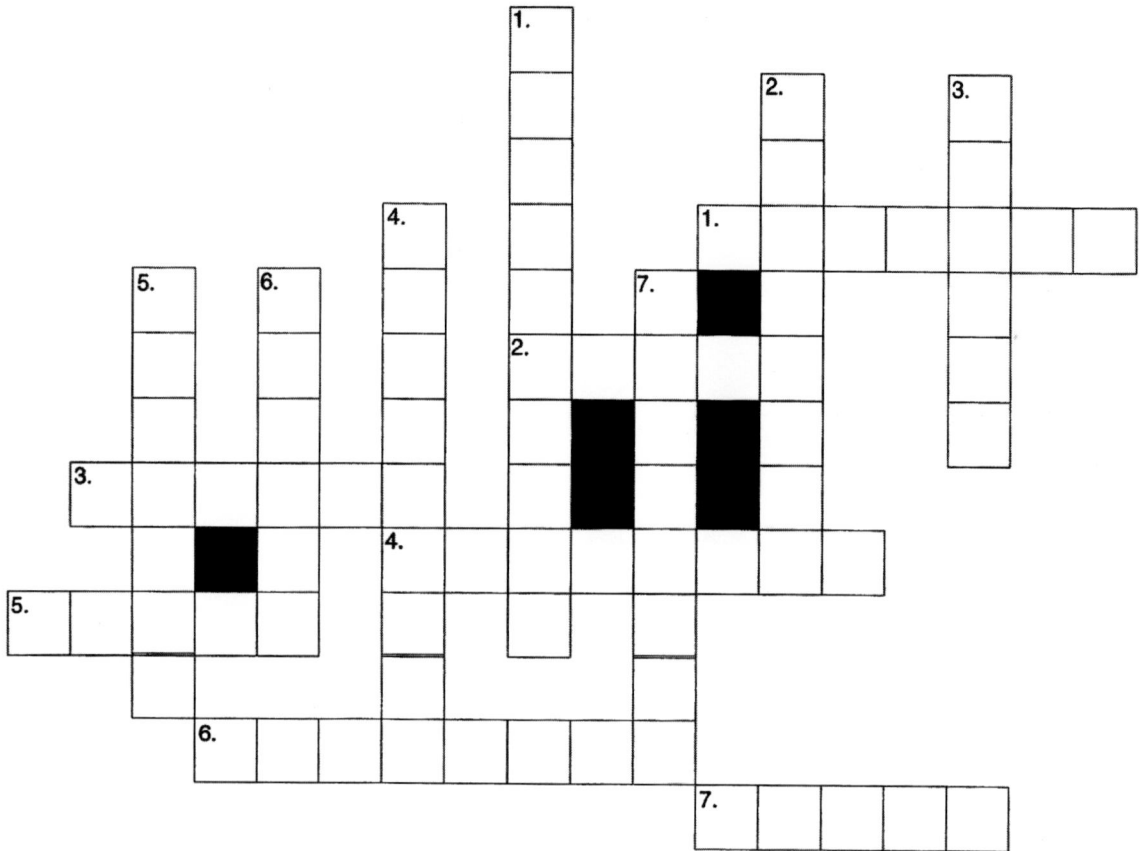

Across:

1. A chase or a hunt.

2. Food, such as apples and oranges.

3. A dark mark which may appear on your skin after it has been hit.

4. Right for a particular purpose or occasion.

5. Liquid produced by a fruit.

6. A container with a lockable lid and a handle for carrying clothes on a journey.

7. Having a lot of juice.

Down:

1. A large, round citrus fruit.

2. Having good results; successful.

3. A gate or door for controlling the flow of water.

4. Worn by an astronaut.

5. Someone who has just joined an organization.

6. A holiday on board a ship.

7. Something which is annoying.

fruit   recruit   pursuit   suitable   fruitful   bruise   suitcase
spacesuit   nuisance   cruise   juicy   sluice   grapefruit   juice

11b

Mixed Bag

ui (oo)

Tailored to Fit

You have been given the word 'suit'. Answer the clues and extend it into longer words.

1. for carrying clothes   suit _ _ _ _

2. worn by an astronaut   _ _ _ _ _ suit

3. right for the occasion   suit _ _ _ _

4. worn when bathing   _ _ _ _ suit

5. not suitable   _ _ suit _ _ _ _

6. noun formed from suitable   suit _ _ _ _ _ _ _

7. someone's interest or regular activity   _ _ _ suit

Words Within Words

Look at the following words. Each word has a hidden word inside it. Solve each clue and write the word which has the answer inside it. The first one has been done for you.

grapefruit   sluice   spacesuit   ~~pursuit~~   juicy   suitable   recruitment   cruise

1. a matching set   p u r s u i t

2. a piece of furniture   _ _ _ _ _ _ _

3. masculine form of 'women'   _ _ _ _ _ _ _ _ _

4. strides   _ _ _ _ _ _ _ _ _

5. frozen water   _ _ _ _ _ _

6. third person singular of the present tense of the verb 'to be'   _ _ _ _ _ _

7. chimpanzee or gorilla   _ _ _ _ _ _ _ _ _ _

8. slippery weather condition   _ _ _ _ _ _

Alphabetical Order

Write the following words in alphabetical order.

suitor   suitability   spacesuit   sluice   suitable   swimsuit   suitcase

_____

_____

Wordsearch

ey (ā)

```
c  o  n  v  e  y  g  r  e  v  e  y  a  r
o  s  o  g  u  v  e  y  g  p  r  i  y  t
n  p  u  r  v  e  y  o  r  e  v  e  y  h
d  r  p  e  a  y  a  b  e  y  a  n  c  e
i  e  d  y  v  t  o  e  y  v  b  s  o  y
s  y  r  h  e  p  u  r  d  e  y  u  d  e
o  s  e  o  y  s  n  e  b  y  p  r  e  y
b  a  s  u  r  v  e  y  o  r  k  v  y  v
e  c  o  n  v  e  y  a  n  c  e  e  b  e
y  e  l  d  r  e  y  d  i  s  e  y  s  y
```

Find each hidden word and write it on the line provided.
Use the LOOK, SAY, COVER, WRITE, CHECK method.

abeyance	_____	osprey	_____
convey	_____	prey	_____
conveyance	_____	purveyor	_____
disobey	_____	survey	_____
drey	_____	surveyor	_____
grey	_____	they	_____
greyhound	_____		

Sound Activities - Extension Exercises

Name............................... Date.....................................

Crossword

ey (ā)

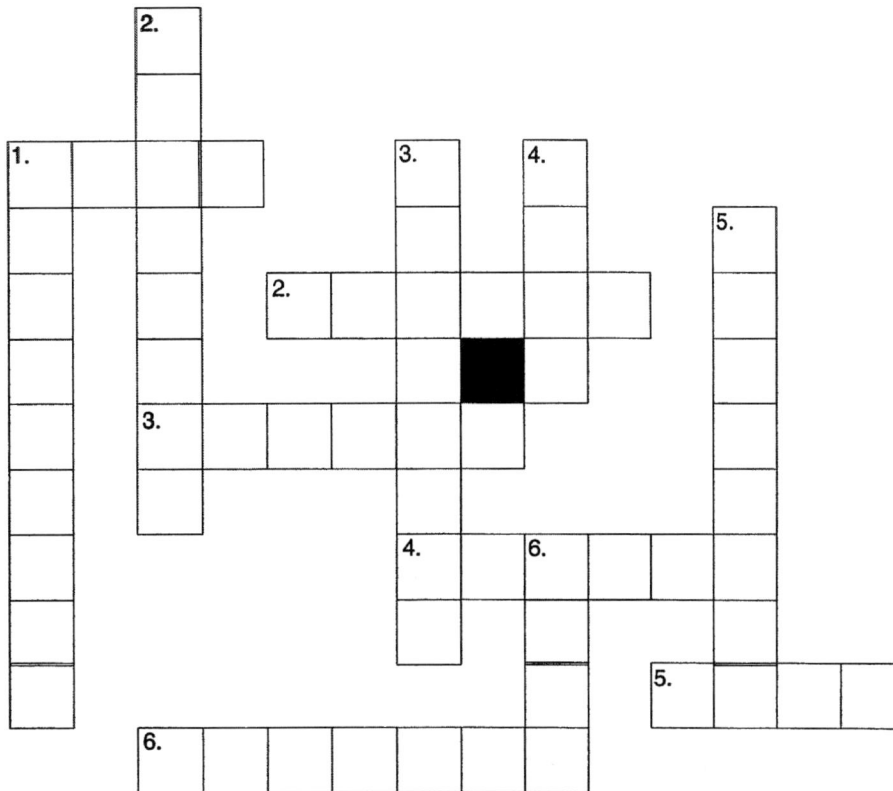

Across:

1. A colour obtained by mixing black and white.

2. To inspect something; to take a general look at something.

3. To carry; transport.

4. A large bird of prey.

5. A squirrel's nest.

6. Opposite of obey.

Down:

1. A breed of dog bred for racing.

2. In the state of being postponed or held over for a time.

3. A person who is in the business of providing or supplying articles of food.

4. The third person plural.

5. A professional person who surveys buildings and land.

6. An animal which is hunted and killed by another animal for food.

| convey | survey | osprey | abeyance | grey | greyhound |
| purveyor | drey | they | prey | disobey | surveyor |

Mixed Bag

ey (ā)

Solve the Riddle

My first is in osprey, but not in prey;   _____

My second in abeyance, but never in conveyance;   _____

My third is in grey as well as in they;   _____

My last's in convey and also in survey.   _____

If you do as you're told, you'll get me easily! The word is _____

Nouns

Write the nouns formed from the following words. Fill in the dashes with the missing letters and write the complete word on the line. If you are not sure, use your dictionary to help you.

1. convey   c o n _ _ _ _ _ _ _   _____

2. obey   o b e _ _ _ _ _ _   _____

3. survey   s u r _ _ _   _____

4. grey   g r e y _ _ _ _   _____

5. disobey   d i s o b e _ _ _ _ _ _   _____

Some General Knowledge Questions

If you are not sure of an answer, use a dictionary, encyclopedia or atlas to help you. Underline the word which has the letters 'ey' (making the long vowel sound 'a') in each question before answering it.

1. What do you call an animal which preys on other animals for food?   P _ _ _ _ _ _ _

2. In which county in the south of England will you find the coastal town
    of Weymouth?   D _ _ _ _ _

3. Which country has Reykavik as its capital city?   I _ _ _ _ _ _

4. In which ocean will you find the islands of Seychelles?   I _ _ _ _ _

5. What does the word 'heyday' mean? _____

    _____

Change a Letter

Starting with the answer to the first clue, change one letter to give the answer of the second and similarly for the third. The answers will have the letter 'ey' (making a long vowel sound 'a') in them.

a colour   _ _ _ _

a squirrel's nest _ _ _ _

a hunted animal   _ _ _ _

Sound Activities - Extension Exercises

Name............................ Date..................................

Wordsearch

```
a  s  t  i  g  c  e  p  o  i  g  n  a  n  t  c  l
w  i  o  g  n  a  r  l  e  d  h  o  m  i  e  o  e
a  g  v  n  a  m  n  d  m  a  l  i  g  n  n  n  n
v  n  m  a  w  p  i  e  k  u  g  p  n  g  g  s  g
e  p  i  s  e  a  s  s  i  g  n  m  e  n  t  i  t
l  o  g  h  d  i  g  i  e  n  g  t  h  e  h  g  h
e  s  n  e  c  g  n  g  c  h  a  m  p  a  g  n  e
n  t  c  k  g  n  e  n  g  t  h  o  l  p  n  m  n
g  f  h  u  s  t  r  e  n  g  t  h  e  n  s  e  r
t  c  o  u  n  t  e  r  s  i  g  n  w  e  g  n  t
h  e  b  e  n  g  t  h  i  m  p  u  g  n  n  t  s
```

Find each hidden word and write it on the line provided.
Use the LOOK, SAY, COVER, WRITE, CHECK method.

assignment	_____	gnawed	_____
campaign	_____	impugn	_____
champagne	_____	lengthen	_____
consignment	_____	malign	_____
countersign	_____	poignant	_____
designer	_____	signpost	_____
gnarled	_____	strengthen	_____
gnash	_____	wavelength	_____

Sound Activities - Extension Exercises

Name.............................. Date...................................

Crossword

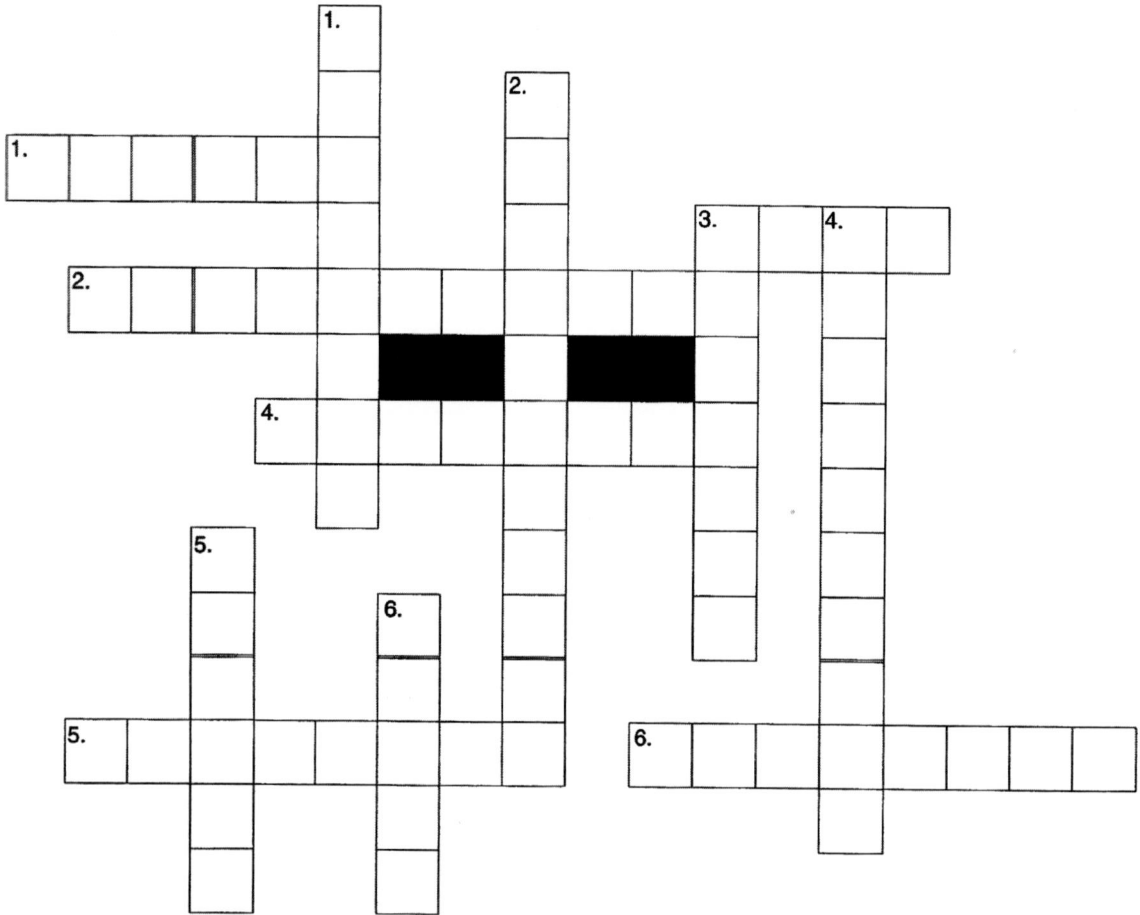

Across:

1. To challenge or question something which has been said or done; to doubt the truth.

2. To sign a document already signed by someone else.

3. To keep on biting something.

4. Someone who makes a pattern or plan of something, which will be made.

5. Affecting the feelings; deeply moving.

6. A sign on a road, giving the name of a place and its distance away.

Down:

1. To make longer.

2. A load or shipment of goods.

3. Twisted and knotty.

4. A task.

5. To say unkind and untrue things about someone.

6. To grind your teeth together.

signpost   lengthen   poignant   impugn   consignment   assignment
designer   malign   countersign   gnarled   gnash   gnaw

13b

Mixed Bag   Silent g

Find the Mystery Word

The following words fit the squares below. Some letters have been given to help you. When you have completed the boxes, a mystery word will be revealed.

consign   lengthen   poignant   strength   designer
              countersign   gnarl   campaign

This will point you in the right direction. The word is _____

Syllables

Splitting a word into its syllables can often help you to spell it. Say each of these words aloud slowly and split it into syllables. You must decide if it has two or three syllables. Write them in the boxes.

	1st	2nd	3rd
countersign			
designer			
strengthen			

	1st	2nd	3rd
consignment			
wavelength			
resign			

Sign Up Here!

You have been given the word 'sign'. Use the following prefixes to solve the clues. Use your dictionary to help you if you are not sure.

de-   re-   con-   en-   as-

1.   to allot or designate   _ _ sign

2.   to hand something over   _ _ _ sign

3.   a pattern   _ _ sign

4.   a military or naval flag   _ _ sign

5.   to give up a job   _ _ sign

Name............................... Date.....................................

Wordsearch

```
a  c  o  u  p  o  n  a  s  t  o  u  y  a
s  m  u  n  y  o  u  t  h  f  u  l  o  u
t  o  a  c  o  u  s  t  i  c  s  o  u  d
o  u  s  o  u  v  e  n  i  r  o  u  t  e
u  s  r  u  o  u  p  t  s  o  u  b  h  l
c  s  e  t  s  i  l  h  o  u  e  t  t  e
a  e  c  h  o  u  f  o  u  t  g  o  u  s
n  k  o  u  g  r  o  u  p  i  c  s  t  i
w  o  u  n  d  o  u  l  e  n  e  m  u  b
d  u  p  c  a  g  o  u  l  e  o  u  v  e
```

Find each hidden word and write it on the line provided.
Use the LOOK, SAY, COVER, WRITE, CHECK method.

acoustics	_____	silhouette	_____
cagoule	_____	soup	_____
coupon	_____	souvenir	_____
group	_____	toucan	_____
mousse	_____	uncouth	_____
recoup	_____	wound	_____
route	_____	youth	_____
routine	_____	youthful	_____

14a

Sound Activities - Extension Exercises

Name.............................. Date....................................

Crossword ou (oo)

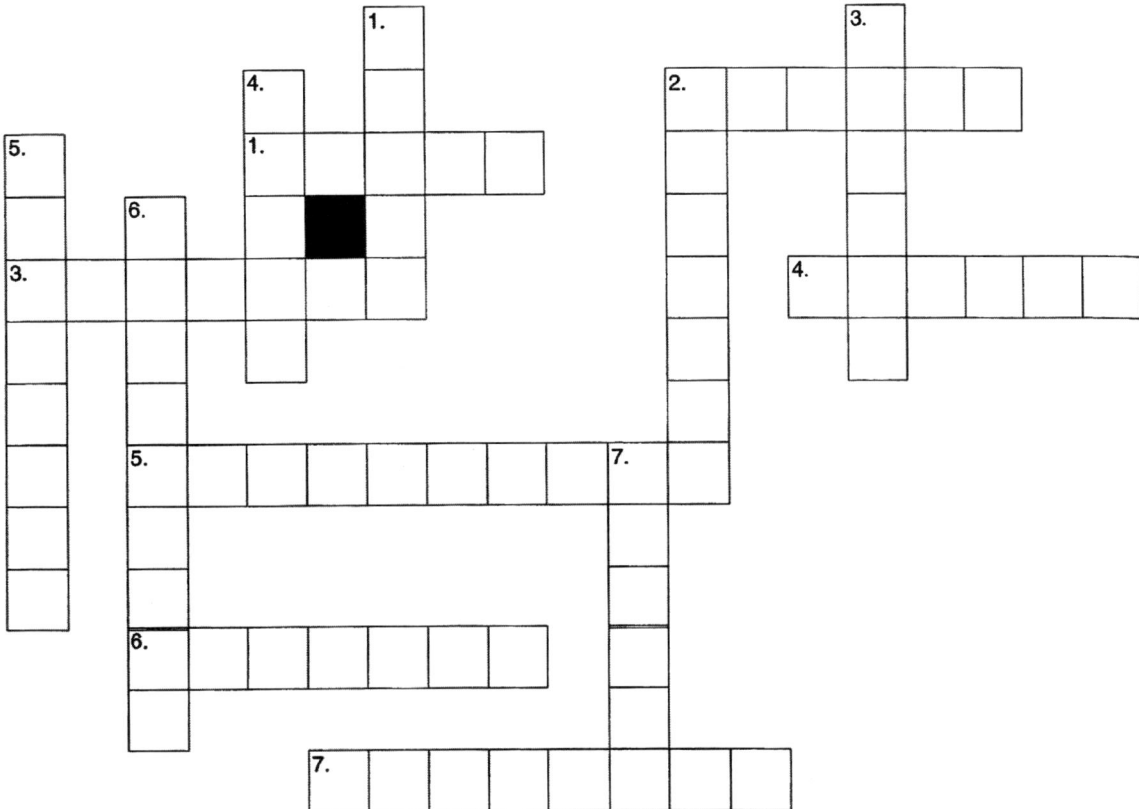

Across:

1. The way you have to follow to get to a place.

2. To recover an amount which has been spent or lost.

3. Rude, rough or vulgar.

4. A frothy cream used for styling hair.

5. A dark outline of a shape seen against a light background.

6. A lightweight, waterproof jacket.

7. Something kept as a reminder of a place.

Down:

1. The early part of life.

2. A regular way of doing something.

3. A ticket used in exchange for something.

4. A number of things together.

5. Young.

6. The qualities making a place good or bad for sound.

7. A tropical bird.

| mousse | cagoule | group | souvenir | toucan | acoustics | youthful |
| youth | routine | route | coupon | silhouette | recoup | uncouth |

14b

Name.............................. Date...................................

Mixed Bag   ou (oo)

What Am I?

My first is twice in mousse, but not at all in group;   _____

There is one in toupee and likewise in soup;   _____

My third is in wound as well as in crouton;   _____

My fourth is in louvre, but never in coupon;   _____

My fifth is once in boutique, but twice in roulette;   _____

My sixth is in toucan, but absent from silhouette;   _____

One appears in acoustics; but none in uncouth;   _____

My last is in routine, but never in youth.   _____

I will remind you of somewhere you have been!   I'm a   _____

Alphabetical Order

Put these words into alphabetical order.
group   youth   routine   coupon   uncouth   cartouche   goulash   you

_____

_____

Anagrams

Rearrange the letters of these anagrams to make the following words.
TOUCAN   SOUVENIR   ROUTINE   ROUTE   SOUP   UNCOUTH
                          SILHOUETTE   ACOUSTICS

1. RUIN TOE   _____   5. A COUNT   _____

2. UNTOUCH   _____   6. OPUS   _____

3. HOTEL SUITE_____   7. SO CAUSTIC _____

4. ONE VIRUS   _____   8. OUTER   _____

Idioms

What do you think these expressions mean? If you do not know try to find out. Use a dictionary of idioms, if you have one.

1.   in the soup _____

      _____

2.   rub salt in the wound _____

      _____

14c

Sound Activities - Extension Exercises

Name.............................   Date...................................

Wordsearch   a (ŏ)

```
q  u  s  q  u  a  r  v  s  q  u  a  d  r  o  n
u  b  q  u  a  l  i  t  y  u  q  u  a  s  i  w
a  s  u  a  d  o  s  q  u  a  l  i  d  q  w  a
r  w  a  l  l  o  w  u  s  n  e  s  q  u  a  t
r  a  n  q  u  a  r  a  n  t  i  n  e  a  r  s
e  d  d  u  w  a  o  l  w  i  w  a  h  b  r  w
l  d  e  a  a  m  k  i  a  t  r  o  m  b  i  a
s  l  r  s  f  w  a  f  f  y  w  a  e  l  o  m
o  e  s  q  t  a  l  y  c  w  a  n  d  e  r  p
m  a  q  u  a  d  r  i  l  a  t  e  r  a  l  e
e  s  q  u  a  q  u  a  n  d  a  r  y  o  n  t
```

Find each hidden word and write it on the line provided.
Use the LOOK, SAY, COVER, WRITE, CHECK method.

quadrilateral   _____   squalid   _____

qualify   _____   squander   _____

quality   _____   squat   _____

quandary   _____   swamp   _____

quantity   _____   waddle   _____

quarantine   _____   waft   _____

quarrelsome   _____   wallow   _____

squabble   _____   wander   _____

squadron   _____   warrior   _____

Sound Activities - Extension Exercises

Crossword

a (ŏ)

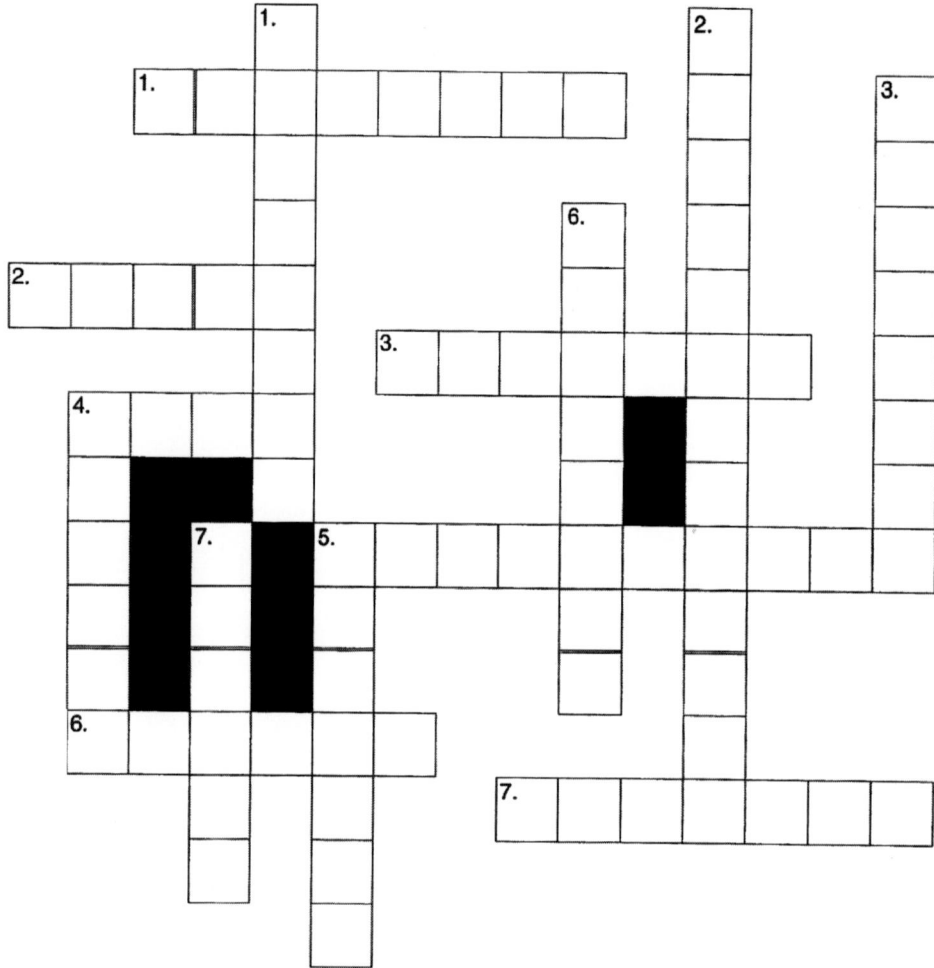

Across:

1. To waste.

2. To sit back on your heels.

3. Dirty and unpleasant.

4. To drift smoothly and lightly through air or over water.

5. A period of isolation for animals or people to stop disease spreading.

6. To walk like a duck.

7. How good or bad something is.

Down:

1. An amount.

2. A shape with four straight sides.

3. To quarrel noisily.

4. To roll about in mud or water.

5. To reach an acceptable standard in order to do a particular job.

6. A puzzling or uncertain situation.

7. To roam.

| squalid | wallow | squander | qualify | waft | quadrilateral | squat |
| quantity | wander | quality | quandary | squabble | quarantine | waddle |

Sound Activities - Extension Exercises

Mixed Bag

a (ŏ)

Words beginning with 'quad'

Can you work out what these words are beginning with 'quad'? Use your dictionary to help you if you are not sure.

1. a four-footed animal   _ _ _ _ _ _ _ _ _ _
2. a four-sided figure   _ _ _ _ _ _ _ _ _ _ _ _
3. a quarter of a circle's circumference   _ _ _ _ _ _ _ _
4. one of four babies born at one birth   _ _ _ _ _ _ _ _ _ _
5. to increase by four times   _ _ _ _ _ _ _ _ _

   So - how many does 'quad' mean?   _____

Odd One Out

Circle the word which is the odd one out and then write why.

swallow   wasp   waffle   wallaby   swan

Reason why _____

Words Within Words

Look at the following words. Each word has a hidden word inside it. Solve each clue and write the word which has the answer inside it. The first one has been done for you.

squalid   swamp   swallow   wallet   wanted   squash   quadrilateral
what   ~~waddle~~   whatever   wander   wasp

1. to find the total of numbers   w a d d l e
2. an insect   _ _ _ _ _ _
3. a top to seal a container   _ _ _ _ _ _
4. opposite of sooner   _ _ _ _ _ _ _ _ _ _
5. past tense of the verb 'to be'   _ _ _ _
6. left after a fire   _ _ _ _ _
7. opposite of love   _ _ _ _ _ _ _
8. past tense of swim   _ _ _ _ _
9. to give permission   _ _ _ _ _ _ _
10. worn on the head   _ _ _ _
11. a barrier of bricks   _ _ _ _ _ _
12. a magic stick   _ _ _ _ _ _

Wordsearch   sc (s followed by soft c)

```
w  e  n  o  s  u  s  c  e  p  t  i  b  l  e  m  k  i
r  t  a  s  c  b  c  d  i  s  c  i  p  l  i  n  e  s
e  r  b  s  e  n  d  i  c  e  a  s  c  e  n  d  s  o
s  u  s  c  n  i  x  f  l  u  s  c  i  o  u  s  c  s
c  s  c  i  e  n  t  i  f  i  c  o  n  p  u  c  r  c
i  c  e  p  a  c  m  f  a  s  c  i  n  a  t  e  e  e
n  i  s  a  d  o  l  e  s  c  e  n  t  s  c  i  s  l
d  m  s  c  i  e  n  s  c  o  n  v  a  l  e  s  c  e
c  o  n  s  c  i  e  n  c  e  d  e  l  i  s  c  e  s
a  m  i  s  c  e  l  l  a  n  e  o  u  s  c  i  n  t
s  c  i  e  n  t  s  c  o  n  s  c  i  o  u  s  t  o
```

Find each hidden word and write it on the line provided.
Use the LOOK, SAY, COVER, WRITE, CHECK method.

abscess	_____	fascinate	_____
adolescent	_____	isosceles	_____
ascend	_____	luscious	_____
conscience	_____	miscellaneous	_____
conscious	_____	rescind	_____
convalesce	_____	scene	_____
crescent	_____	scientific	_____
discipline	_____	susceptible	_____

Sound Activities - Extension Exercises

Crossword   sc (s followed by soft c)

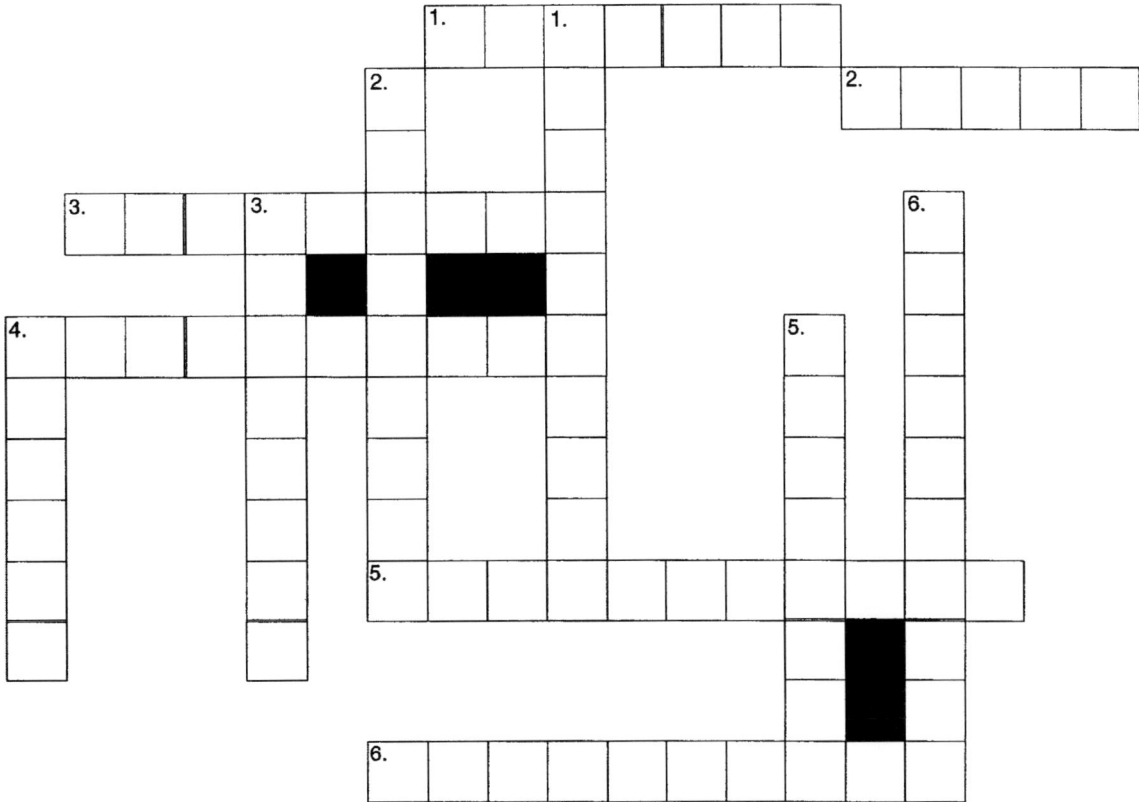

Across:

1. To cancel or withdraw.

2. The place where something happens.

3. To attract and charm.

4. A young person who is older than a child, but not yet an adult.

5. Easily affected; sensitive to something.

6. To recover after an illness.

Down:

1. To do with science.

2. Aware of something.

3. A shape like a new moon.

4. To go up.

5. Tasting or smelling delicious.

6. Self-control; obedience.

scientific   susceptible   discipline   adolescent   scene
crescent   ascend   conscious   rescind   luscious   convalesce   fascinate

Name............................... Date....................................

Mixed Bag
sc (s followed by soft c)

Consonants and Vowels

You have been given the vowels of the following words. Fill in the missing consonants and write the complete word on the line.

adolescent   fascinate   conscience   discipline   luscious   isosceles

1.   _ o _ _ _ i e _ _ e   _____

2.   _ u _ _ i o u _   _____

3.   a _ o _ e _ _ e _ _   _____

4.   i _ o _ _ e _ e _   _____

5.   _ a _ _ i _ a _ e   _____

6.   _ i _ _ i _ _ i _ e   _____

What goes up, must come down!

You have been given the word 'descend'. Now build the following words around it.

scenery   rescind   discern   scissors   descendant   crescent   convalesce

```
1.|   |   |   |   |   |   | d |   |   |   |
                          2.| e |   |   |   |   |
                      3.|   | s |   |   |
                    4.|   |   | c |   |
                    5.|   |   |   | e |   |
                        6.|   |   | n |   |   |   |   |
                              7.| d |   |   |   |   |   |
```

Definitions

Use your dictionary to find the meaning of each of these words.

1.   discern _____

_____

2.   descendant _____

_____

Some General Knowledge Questions

1.   What is an isosceles triangle?_____

2.   What is a scimitar? _____

3.   What is the name of the islands west of the tip of Cornwall in the south-west of England?

_____

16c

Name............................... Date....................................

Wordsearch

ch (sh)

```
s  o  m  c  p  a  s  n  d  c  h  u  t  e  w
c  h  c  h  a  r  a  d  e  h  i  g  c  m  e
h  a  m  z  r  o  c  h  e  a  c  h  s  o  r
i  p  a  n  a  c  h  e  c  n  h  b  r  u  i
v  b  c  h  c  h  e  w  h  d  l  c  a  s  c
a  r  h  c  h  e  t  c  r  e  c  h  e  t  o
l  o  i  q  u  i  c  h  e  l  h  o  m  a  c
r  c  n  u  t  r  h  e  c  i  c  h  i  c  h
o  h  e  i  e  c  u  f  h  e  h  v  c  h  e
u  u  m  a  c  h  i  n  e  r  y  c  h  e  t
s  r  o  c  h  c  h  a  u  f  f  e  u  r  o
p  e  d  c  h  a  l  e  t  i  g  t  c  h  s
```

Find each hidden word and write it on the line provided.
Use the LOOK, SAY, COVER, WRITE, CHECK method.

brochure _____   creche _____

chalet _____   machine _____

chandelier _____   machinery _____

charade _____   moustache _____

chauffeur _____   panache _____

chef _____   parachute _____

chic _____   quiche _____

chivalrous _____   ricochet _____

chute _____   sachet _____

Note: 'chalet' is pronounced 'shalay'; 'ricochet' - 'ricoshay'; 'sachet' - 'sashay'

Name............................. Date...................................

Crossword

ch (sh)

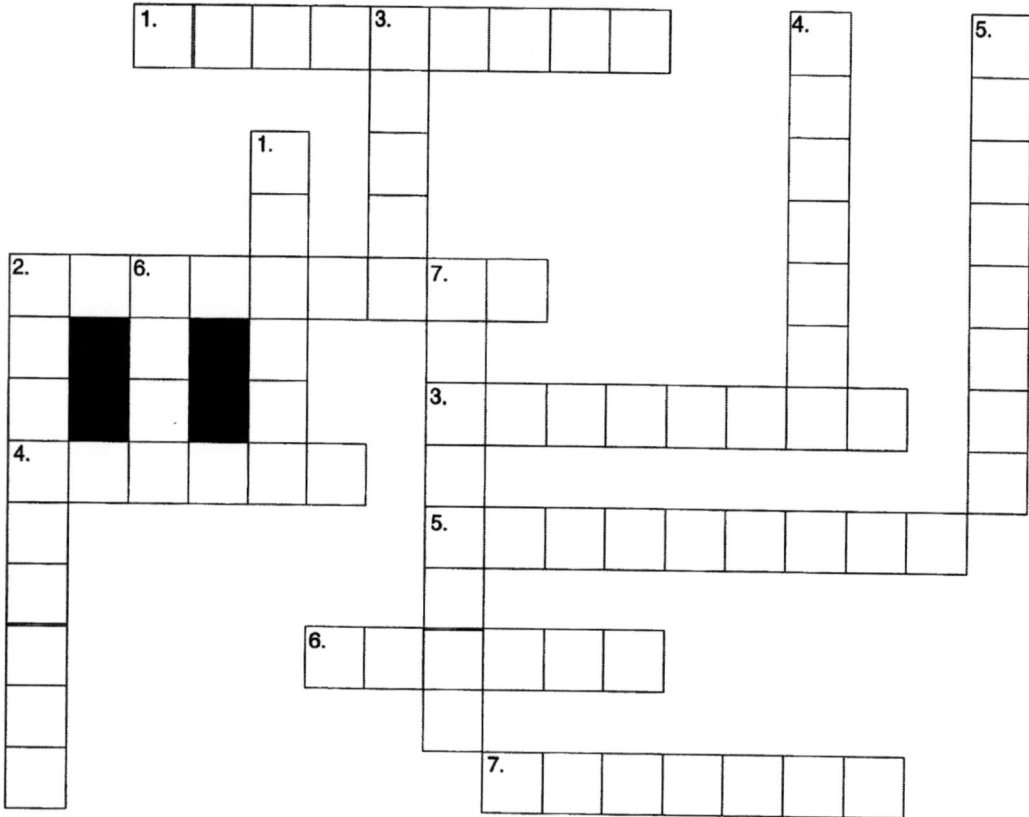

Across:

1. An umbrella - shaped device enabling a person to come safely to earth from a great height.

2. The parts of a machine.

3. A game - guessing a word from another person's actions.

4. A small, sealed envelope or packet containing something, such as shampoo.

5. Someone who drives a car for someone else.

6. A place where parents can leave very young children, while they are busy.

7. Dashing style.

Down:

1. An open, savoury tart.

2. A growth of hair above a man's upper lip.

3. A sloping channel forming a slide.

4. A set of parts working together to do a job.

5. A pamphlet containing information.

6. Smart; very fashionable.

7. Rebounding off a surface; such as a bullet rebounding off a rock.

chauffeur   machine   quiche   creche   machinery   chic   ricochet
chute   moustache   parachute   brochure   sachet   charades   panache

17b

Name............................. Date...................................

Mixed Bag   ch (sh)

Some General Knowledge Questions

Underline the word in each question which contains the letters 'ch' (making a 'sh' sound) before answering it. Use a dictionary or an encyclopedia to help you if you are not sure of the answers.

1. In which American state would you find the city of Chicago?   I _ _ _ _ _ _ _

2. What would you do with a 'chaise longue'? a) read it;   b) eat it;   c) sit on it
    _____

3. What does a 'chef' do? _____

4. What type of animal is a 'chamois' (pronounced 'shamwah')?   A _ _ _ _ _ _ _ _

5. Where in a room might you find a 'chandelier'? _____

6. What type of food is a 'pistachio'?_____

7. Who was Frederic Chopin? a) an artist;   b) a poet;   c) a composer;   d) a writer
    _____

8. 'Charlotte' is the feminine form of which masculine name? _____

9. Would you trust a 'charlatan'? Give a reason for your answer._____
    _____

How Revealing!

Use the following words to answer the clues. If you answer correctly, a mystery word will be revealed.

brochure   sachet   pistachio   chef   Charlotte   chic   moustache
chalet   quiche

1. a kind of nut

2. a girl's name

3. a leaflet

4. a packet

5. very fashionable

6. a mountain hut

7. a savoury tart

8. hair above the top lip

9. a cook

This will bring you back down to earth! It's a_____

Wordsearch

eu (ū)

```
r e p h a r m a c e u t i c a l r
o s n e u t r a l u t n e u t r h
p n e u m a t i c p n e u f u b e
h e u r s t e u p h e m i s m e u
e r m h f e u r h o u z s a s t m
u h o f e u n e u r o t i c l e a
s o n e u t r a l i z e s r e n t
t r i u d o n i m a t u n e u f i
e p a s t e u r i z e l m u t n s
a k u t h e r a p e u t i c h t m
```

Find each hidden word and write it on the line provided.
Use the LOOK, SAY, COVER, WRITE, CHECK method.

euphemism _____   pharmaceutical _____

euphoria _____   pneumatic _____

feud _____   pneumonia _____

neurotic _____   rheumatism _____

neutral _____   sleuth _____

neutralize _____   therapeutic _____

pasteurize _____

18a

Name............................... Date....................................

Crossword

eu (ū)

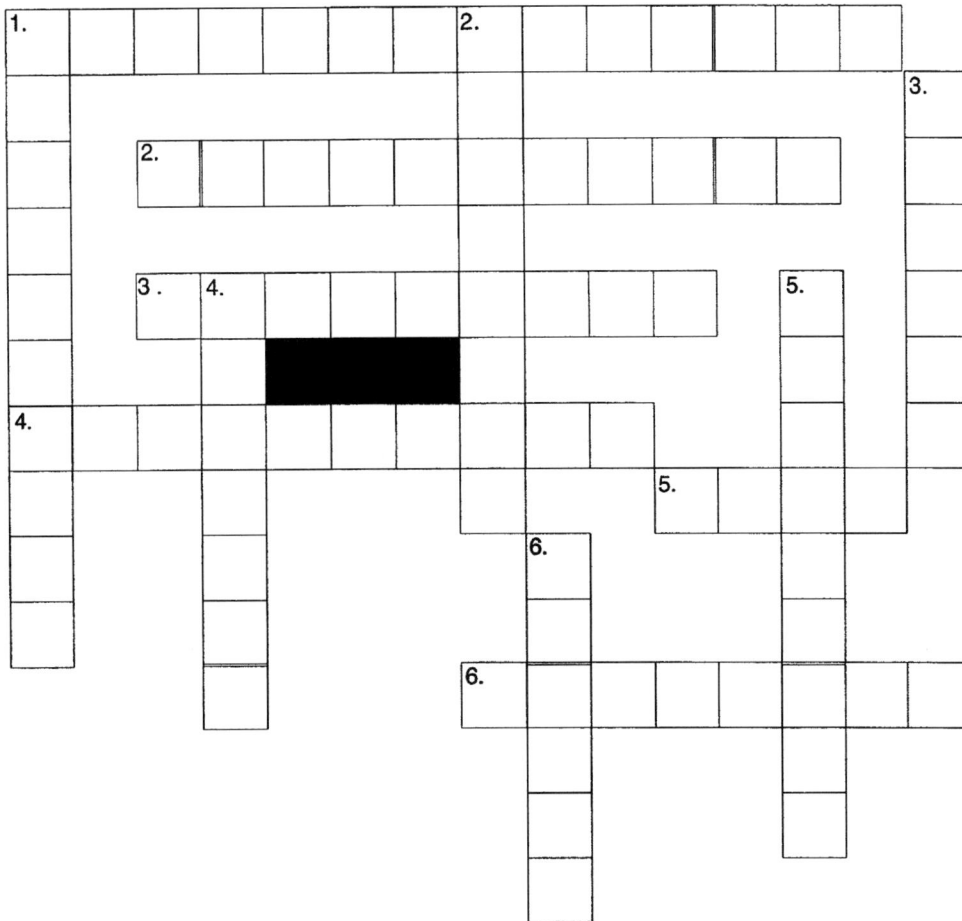

Across:

1. To do with the making and dispensing of medicines.

2. Treating an illness by having a calming and relaxing effect.

3. Inflammation of the lungs.

4. A disease causing stiffness and pain in the joints of the body.

5. Long-lasting quarrel between people, families, tribes, etc.

6. Constantly being very worried and anxious about something.

Down:

1. To purify milk and make it safe to drink by heating it and then cooling it.

2. A feeling of great happiness.

3. Britain and France are part of this continent.

4. Not supporting either side in a quarrel or a war.

5. Worked by compressed air, such as a drill used for road-works.

6. A detective.

| pneumonia | euphoria | pharmaceutical | sleuth | neurotic | pneumatic |
| pasteurize | neutral | Europe | feud | rheumatism | therapeutic |

Name.............................. Date...................................

Mixed Bag

eu (ū)

Nouns and Adjectives

Complete the columns with either the noun or the adjective.
If you are not sure, use your dictionary to help you.

Noun	Adjective
pharmacy	
	therapeutic
Europe	
	euphoric
neurosis	
	rheumatic

Some General Knowledge Questions

Underline the word in each question which contains the letters 'eu' in it before answering it. Use a dictionary or an encyclopedia to help you if you are not sure of the answers.

1. Who wrote the books about the sleuth, Sherlock Holmes? _____

2. What would you do with a 'euphonium'? a) speak to someone through it;

   b) play a tune on it; c) plant it in the garden. _____

3. The process of pasteurizing milk is named after the person who discovered it. What was

   his name? _____

4. What is a 'eucalyptus'? a) a fish; b) a bird; c) a tree; d) a vegetable. _____

5. In which continent is the Euphrates River?_____

Definitions

Use your dictionary to find the meaning of each of these words.

1. euphemism _____

   _____

2. eulogy _____

   _____

3. neurology _____

   _____

18c

Name............................. Date....................................

Wordsearch   Silent letters (b, h, s, w)

```
c  a  w  d  o  u  t  e  d  r  o  v  m  b  d
h  w  r  e  c  k  a  g  e  l  w  a  i  k  o
a  r  e  b  a  r  h  u  b  a  r  b  w  e  u
s  i  w  r  i  n  g  b  t  h  i  w  r  t  b
s  t  r  i  s  l  a  n  d  i  n  g  h  y  t
i  h  i  s  l  o  m  b  i  s  e  h  y  m  f
s  e  p  d  e  c  i  s  u  c  c  u  m  b  u
d  u  m  b  f  o  u  n  d  e  d  n  e  t  l
f  w  r  a  p  p  e  r  g  h  a  s  t  l  y
```

Find each hidden word and write it on the line provided.
Use the LOOK, SAY, COVER, WRITE, CHECK method.

debt _____   aisle _____

doubtful _____   chassis _____

dumbfounded _____   debris _____

succumb _____   island _____

dinghy _____   wrapper _____

ghastly _____   wreckage _____

rhubarb _____   wring _____

rhyme _____   writhe _____

Crossword   Silent letters (b, h, s, w)

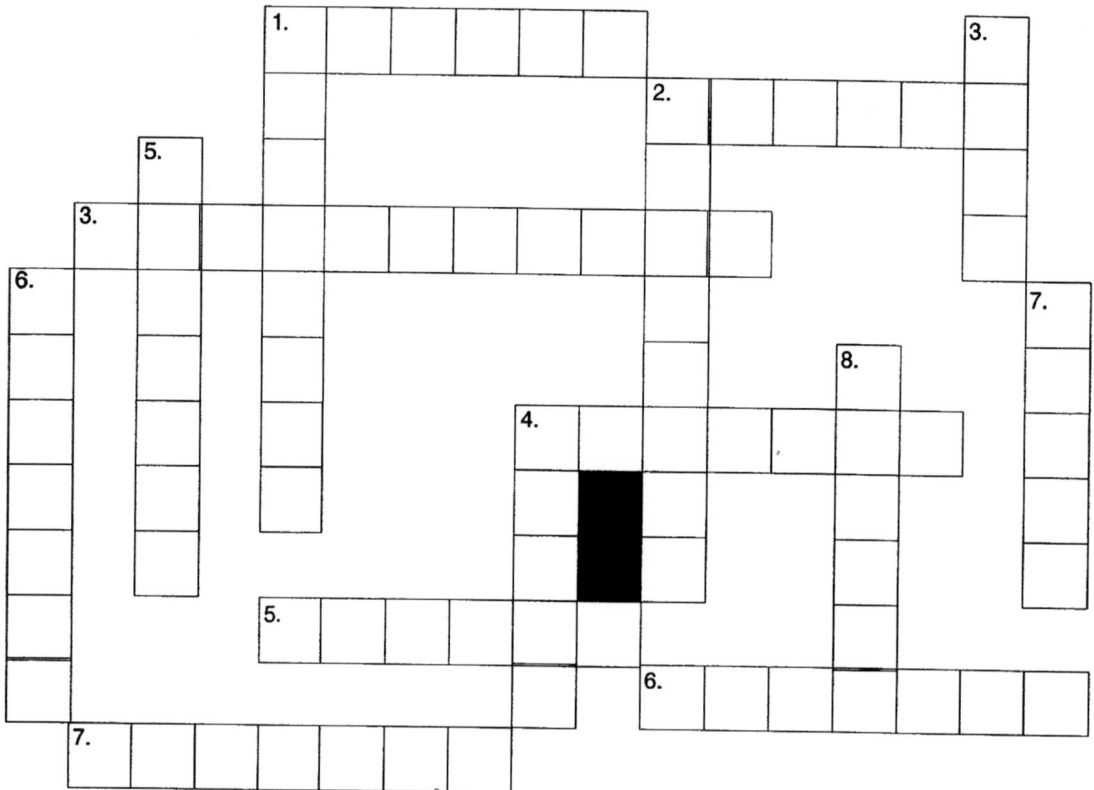

Across:

1. A small rowing boat.

2. To twist and roll about when in pain.

3. Unable to speak because of being so surprised and astonished.

4. A piece of paper around something such as a sweet.

5. An area of land surrounded by water.

6. Awful; terrible

7. A plant which has green or pink stalks used as a fruity filling for a pie.

Down:

1. Unsure about something.

2. The remaining pieces of a car, ship and so on, which has been destroyed.

3. Something which is owed to someone.

4. To twist and squeeze something using force.

5. To be forced to give way to something.

6. The metal frame and wheels of a vehicle, supporting the body.

7. A passage between rows of seats.

8. Scattered fragments of wreckage.

rhubarb   wreckage   aisle   wrapper   succumb   ghastly   debt   dinghy
dumbfounded   wring   debris   writhe   doubtful   chassis   island

Name.............................   Date....................................

Mixed Bag   Silent letters (b, h, s, w)

The Silent Majority

Many of the following words have silent letters in them. You have to decide which they are.
Write each one down and circle the silent letter. The first one has been done for you.

g̶h̶o̶s̶t̶	wriggle	wisest	honour	thirsty	landing
island	growth	faster	debris	speech	doubt
comb	wicket	succumb	wrapper	spring	wring
analysis	chassis	basis	rhythm		

_____ g (h) o s t _____   _____

_____   _____

_____   _____

_____   _____

_____   _____

_____   _____

Confusing Words

Look carefully at these two words and how they are spelt. What does each word mean? Use
your dictionary to help you if you are not sure.

dinghy _____

dingy_____

Why does 'dinghy' have a hard 'g' sound and 'dingy' a soft 'g' sound?

Reason: _____

Anagrams

Rearrange the letters of these anagrams to make the following words.

ISLANDS   SHIPWRECKED   RHYME   AISLES   WRECKAGE
RHINOCEROS   WRESTLE   WRITHES   WRAPPING   DEBRIS

1. MR HEY   _____   6. BRIDES   _____

2. SS LINDA   _____   7. CRAG WEEK   _____

3. WITHERS   _____   8. CORNISH ORE   _____

4. LASSIE   _____   9. DECK WHISPER   _____

5. PRAWN PIG   _____   10. SWELTER   _____

Mnemonics

Mnemonics are ways of helping you to remember things.

Here is a good way of remembering how to spell 'island'.

An island 'IS LAND' surrounded by water.

19c

Sound Activities - Extension Exercises

Name.............................. Date...................................

Wordsearch

```
t  o  r  p  e  d  i  g  r  e  e  s  c  e  e
f  l  e  e  n  o  s  j  e  e  c  t  h  m  j
l  a  f  a  m  d  c  u  f  l  o  a  i  i  a
e  d  e  g  r  e  e  b  u  w  m  p  m  r  m
s  p  r  e  e  c  e  i  g  e  m  s  p  q  b
p  o  e  e  e  r  s  l  e  e  i  g  a  u  o
l  s  e  t  t  e  e  e  e  c  t  l  n  e  r
e  d  f  o  r  e  s  e  e  h  t  e  z  e  e
e  a  z  u  v  m  a  r  q  u  e  e  e  l  e
s  g  u  a  r  a  n  t  e  e  e  t  e  e  m
c  o  f  f  e  e  b  z  e  t  o  f  f  e  e
```

Find each hidden word and write it on the line provided.
Use the LOOK, SAY, COVER, WRITE, CHECK method.

chimpanzee	_____	jamboree	_____
coffee	_____	jubilee	_____
committee	_____	marquee	_____
decree	_____	pedigree	_____
degree	_____	referee	_____
flee	_____	refugee	_____
foresee	_____	settee	_____
glee	_____	spree	_____
guarantee	_____	toffee	_____

Sound Activities - Extension Exercises

Name............................. Date.................................

Crossword

- ee

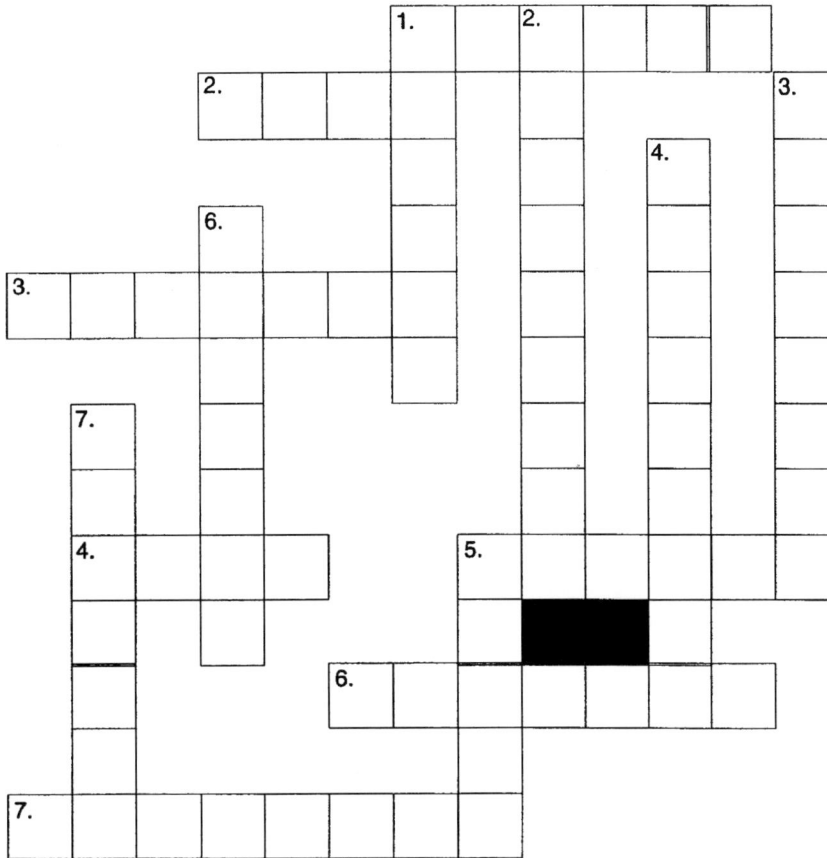

Across:

1. A unit of measurement of angles and temperature.

2. Delight.

3. A person seeking shelter in another country from danger in his or her own country.

4. To run away.

5. A sofa.

6. A very large tent.

7. A list of a person's or animal's parents and ancestors.

Down:

1. An official order given by a court of law.

2. A promise to replace or repair bought goods, if they are unsatisfactory.

3. A celebration; a large gathering of Scouts.

4. A group of people appointed to do a special job.

5. A fun shopping trip when many things are bought.

6. A joyful celebration of an anniversary.

7. The person controlling a football match.

settee   **referee**   guarantee   spree   jamboree   decree   flee   refugee
degree   **pedigree**   committee   jubilee   marquee   glee

Sound Activities - Extension Exercises

Mixed Bag

- ee

The Suffix '-ee'

The suffix '-ee' is used for someone who is involved in something or who is subjected to something.

For example: an 'evacuee' is someone who has to evacuate (leave) his or her home to avoid danger during a war.

Match the word with its meaning.

absentee   nominee   referee   trainee   employee   trustee

1.   Someone who makes sure a game is played by the rules is a   _____

2.   Someone who looks after money entrusted to him or her is a   _____

3.   Someone who is not present at an event is an   _____

4.   Someone who works for someone else is an   _____

5.   Someone who is being taught to do a job is a   _____

6.   Someone who has his or her name put forward for something is a   _____

Idioms

Match each expression with its meaning.

Idiom	Meaning
to see red	to have no responsibilities
can't do something for toffee	to escape punishment
something doesn't grow on trees	to wait to see how a situation develops
to bark up the wrong tree	to become very angry
to go down on bended knee	to be very bad at doing something
to be footloose and fancy free	to allow someone freedom of action
to see which way the cat jumps	to follow a wrong course of action
to get off scot-free	to beg for something
to give someone a free rein	something is very scarce

Name.............................. Date...............................

Wordsearch

-eous

```
b  o  u  n  c  e  o  u  s  b  o  u  n  t  e  o  u  s
s  d  s  a  h  h  i  d  e  o  u  s  b  r  c  v  p  m
i  o  p  u  u  n  e  o  u  s  o  v  o  i  o  r  i  i
m  m  i  s  c  e  l  l  a  n  e  o  u  s  u  a  t  n
u  l  l  e  o  u  s  p  o  n  s  u  t  a  r  r  e  g
l  s  p  o  n  t  a  n  e  o  u  s  r  c  t  g  o  a
t  t  o  u  t  i  n  s  t  a  n  t  a  n  e  o  u  s
a  r  c  s  e  o  u  s  p  r  o  n  g  e  o  r  s  e
n  e  r  r  o  n  e  o  u  s  h  f  e  o  u  g  e  o
e  o  o  i  s  u  r  i  g  h  t  e  o  u  s  e  o  u
o  u  n  l  c  o  u  r  a  g  e  o  u  s  e  o  u  s
u  s  b  c  i  f  r  i  m  e  o  u  s  k  t  u  s  t
s  a  d  v  a  n  t  a  g  e  o  u  s  e  n  s  h  m
```

Find each hidden word and write it on the line provided.
Use the LOOK, SAY, COVER, WRITE, CHECK method.

advantageous _____	instantaneous _____
bounteous _____	miscellaneous _____
courageous _____	nauseous _____
courteous _____	outrageous _____
erroneous _____	piteous _____
gaseous _____	righteous _____
gorgeous _____	simultaneous _____
hideous _____	spontaneous _____

Name............................... Date...................................

Crossword

-eous

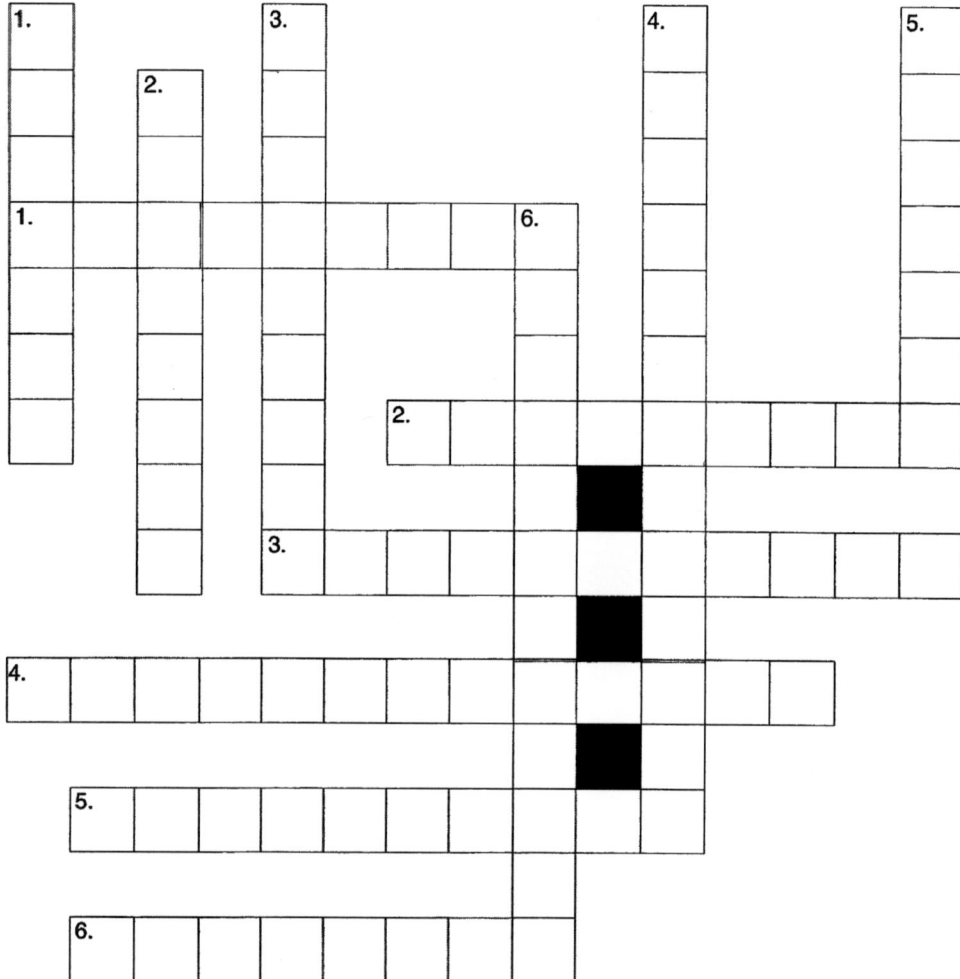

Across:

1. Incorrect.

2. Polite.

3. Happening or done naturally without being prompted.

4. Mixed; various.

5. Brave.

6. Causing a feeling of sickness.

Down:

1. Causing pity.

2. Magnificent; beautiful.

3. Freely given; in abundance.

4. Happening instantly.

5. Horribly ugly.

6. Happening at the same time.

spontaneous   gorgeous   courageous   instantaneous   piteous   hideous
erroneous   simultaneous   miscellaneous   bounteous   nauseous   courteous

Sound Activities - Extension Exercises

Name.............................. Date....................................

Mixed Bag

-eous

Nouns and Adjectives

Complete the columns with either the noun or the adjective.
If you are not sure, use your dictionary to help you.

Noun	Adjective
	outrageous
	instantaneous
gas	
courage	
	piteous
error	
	miscellaneous
righteousness	
	nauseous
	spontaneous
advantage	

Words Within Words

Solve the clue and write the word from the following list which has the answer inside it. The first
one has been done for you.

hideous	miscellaneous	piteous	gorgeous	~~spontaneous~~
nauseous	courteous	outrageous	righteous	advantageous

1. a light brown colour   <u>s</u> <u>p</u> <u>o</u> <u>n</u> <u>t</u> <u>a</u> <u>n</u> <u>e</u> <u>o</u> <u>u</u> <u>s</u>

2. violent anger   _ _ _ _ _ _ _ _ _

3. to conceal   _ _ _ _ _ _ _

4. opposite of left   _ _ _ _ _ _ _ _

5. where tennis is played   _ _ _ _ _ _ _ _

6. to utilize   _ _ _ _ _ _ _ _

7. a room in a prison   _ _ _ _ _ _ _ _ _ _ _ _

8. a deep hole in the ground   _ _ _ _ _ _ _

9. to eat greedily   _ _ _ _ _ _ _ _

10. a motor vehicle   _ _ _ _ _ _ _ _ _ _ _

Name.............................. Date...................................

Wordsearch

s	m	l	u	m	e	a	g	r	e	l	r	e	c	t
m	i	o	g	r	e	r	c	a	l	i	b	r	e	i
a	l	u	s	t	r	e	e	g	a	t	m	e	n	g
n	l	v	r	e	v	r	n	b	r	r	a	f	t	m
o	i	r	e	n	m	e	t	r	e	e	c	i	i	a
e	m	e	d	i	o	c	r	e	u	w	a	b	m	s
u	e	n	r	e	t	u	e	s	o	m	b	r	e	s
v	t	h	e	a	t	r	e	m	a	c	r	e	t	a
r	r	a	e	p	i	c	e	n	t	r	e	p	r	c
e	e	p	l	r	e	h	o	s	r	e	r	r	e	r
c	e	n	r	e	s	k	i	l	o	m	e	t	r	e

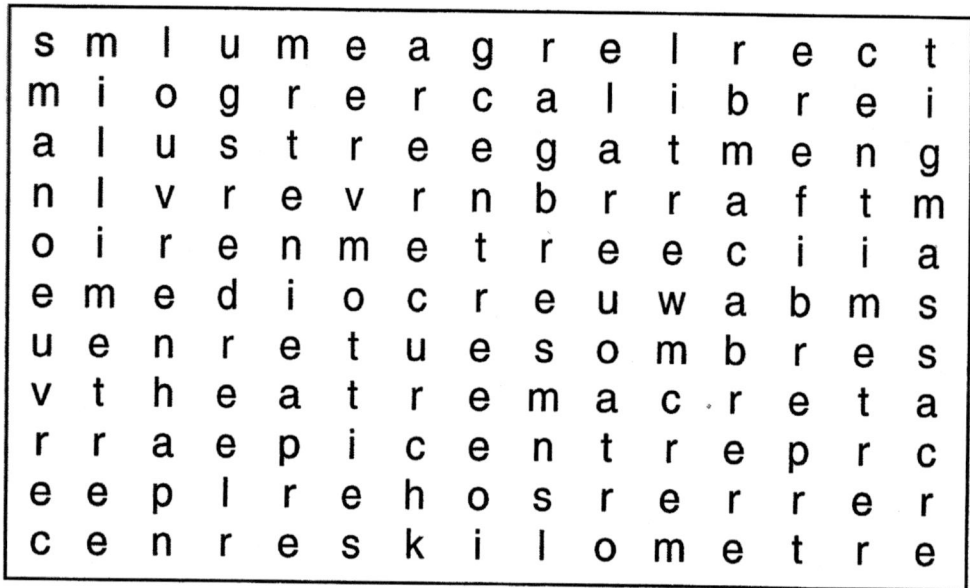

Find each hidden word and write it on the line provided.
Use the LOOK, SAY, COVER, WRITE, CHECK method.

acre _____   macabre _____

calibre _____   manoeuvre _____

centimetre _____   massacre _____

centre _____   meagre _____

epicentre _____   mediocre _____

fibre _____   metre _____

kilometre _____   millimetre _____

litre _____   ogre _____

louvre _____   sombre _____

lustre _____   theatre _____

22a

Sound Activities - Extension Exercises

Name.............................. Date.................................

Crossword

-re

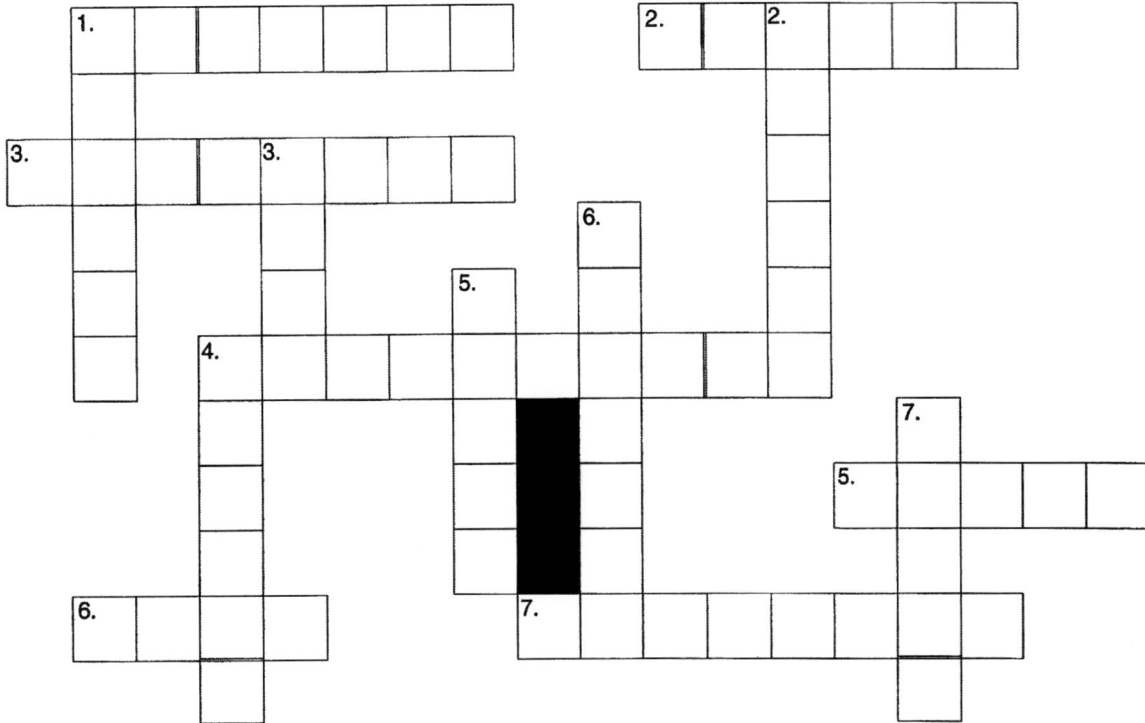

Across:

1. Strange; gruesome; horrible.

2. Brilliance; the shine on a surface.

3. The killing of a large number of people.

4. Ten millimetres.

5. A measure of liquid.

6. A cruel giant in stories.

7. Only being fairly good; second-rate.

Down:

1. Very little of something; hardly enough.

2. Dark or gloomy.

3. An area of land of about 4000 square metres (4840 square yards).

4. The middle of something.

5. A thin thread.

6. A building in which a play is performed.

7. A bishop's hat.

| centimetre | acre | litre | mediocre | theatre | meagre | mitre |
| fibre | massacre | centre | lustre | ogre | macabre | sombre |

Name............................... Date.......................................

Mixed Bag

-re

Some General Knowledge Questions

Use a dictionary or encyclopedia to help you if you are not sure of the answers. Underline the word or words ending in 're' in each question before answering it.

1. How many centimetres are there in a metre? _____

2. Who would wear a mitre on the head? _____

3. In which city in France would you find the famous Louvre

   museum and art gallery? _____

4. What type of weapon is a sabre? _____

5. What is measured in acres? _____

6. What is the line called which goes from the centre of a circle to its edge? _____

7. How many decimetres are in a metre? _____

8. How many metres are in a decametre? _____

Nouns and Adjectives

Complete the columns with either the noun or the adjective.
If you are not sure, use your dictionary to help you.

Noun	Adjective
fibre	
	central
theatre	
	mediocre
lustre	
	ogrish

Homophones

What is the difference in meaning between 'metre' and 'meter'? Use your dictionary to help you if you are not sure.

metre:_____

meter : _____

Sound Activities - Extension Exercises

Name............................. Date.................................

Wordsearch -que

```
s  t  a  m  b  u  b  o  u  t  i  q  u  e  t  u
t  r  i  y  o  p  a  q  u  e  b  c  n  i  g  v
a  m  o  s  q  u  e  u  m  c  r  l  i  a  r  u
t  u  b  t  o  c  f  e  i  h  u  o  q  n  o  p
u  s  l  i  q  h  e  d  p  n  s  q  u  t  t  h
e  p  i  q  u  e  q  c  l  i  q  u  e  i  e  y
s  l  q  u  e  q  u  e  a  q  u  e  c  q  s  s
q  a  u  e  q  u  e  l  q  u  e  k  r  u  q  i
u  g  e  s  p  e  c  q  u  e  n  i  v  e  u  q
e  d  i  s  c  o  t  h  e  q  u  e  c  k  e  u
s  e  q  u  e  p  i  c  t  u  r  e  s  q  u  e
```

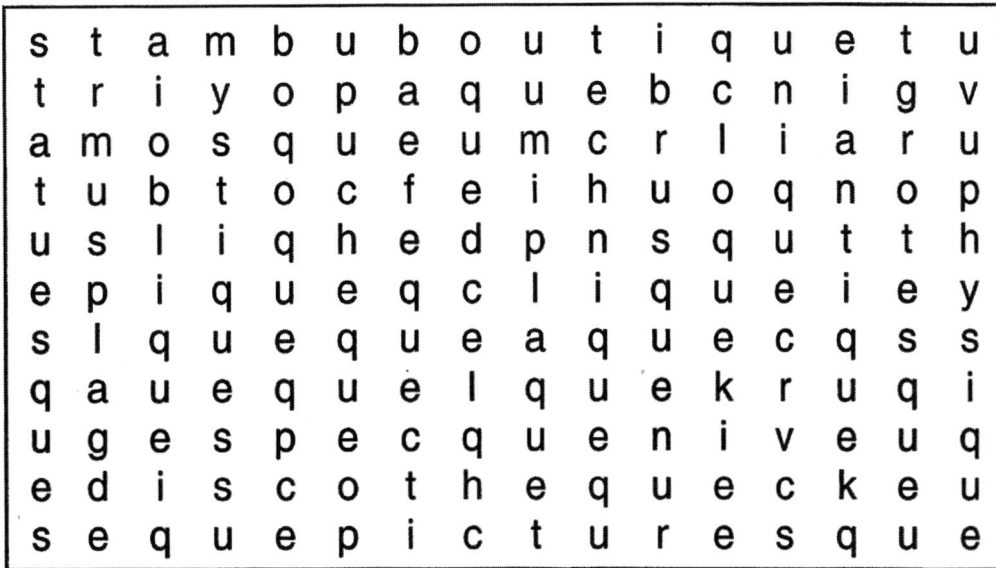

Find each hidden word and write it on the line provided.
Use the LOOK, SAY, COVER, WRITE, CHECK method.

antique   _____   oblique   _____

boutique   _____   opaque   _____

brusque   _____   physique   _____

cheque   _____   picturesque   _____

clique   _____   pique   _____

discotheque   _____   plaque   _____

grotesque   _____   statuesque   _____

mosque   _____   technique   _____

mystique   _____   unique   _____

23a

Name............................... Date...................................

Crossword

-que

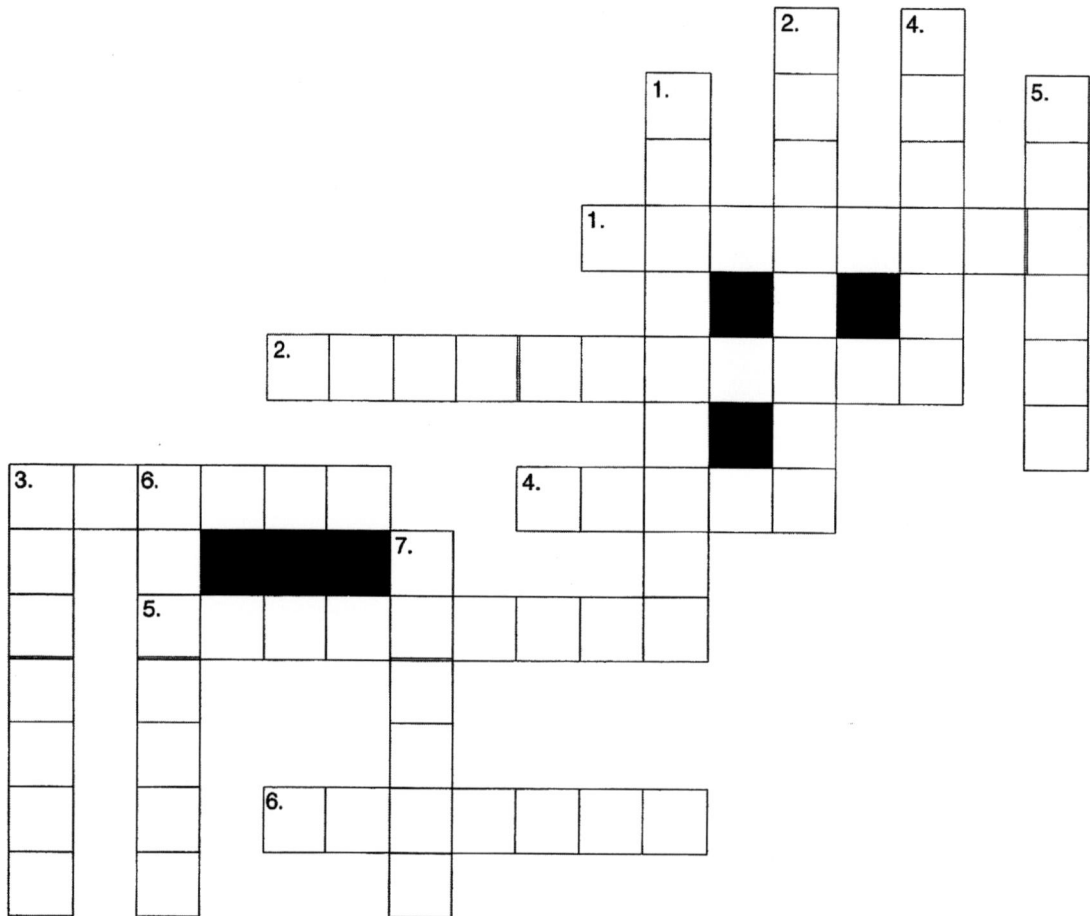

Across:

1. A small shop selling fashionable clothes.

2. Attractive or charming appearance.

3. Not transparent.

4. A hurt or offended feeling.

5. A way of doing something.

6. Having a blunt or offhand manner.

Down:

1. Very strange and ugly.

2. An atmosphere of mystery.

3. Slanting; greater or less than a right angle.

4. A mounted plate with engraved words on it.

5. A written order to a banker to pay money from someone's account.

6. An old and valuable object.

7. Being the only one of its kind.

antique   cheque   picturesque   unique   oblique   technique   pique
opaque   grotesque   plaque   brusque   mystique   boutique

23b

Mixed Bag
-que

Synonyms and Antonyms

From the following list of words, find a synonym (similar meaning) and an antonym (opposite meaning) for each word in the box. If you are not sure, use your dictionary or thesaurus to help you.

slanting   modern   polite   straight   unequalled   old
transparent   charming   repulsive   common   clouded   abrupt

		Synonym	Antonym
1.	opaque		
2.	grotesque		
3.	unique		
4.	brusque		
5.	antique		
6.	oblique		

What's in a Word?

Use your dictionary to find out about these words.

1. A 'disco' is where people go to dance to recorded pop music, but it comes from a longer word which comes from the French language. Can you find out what the longer word is?

_____

2. What kind of dancing would you be doing if you performed an 'arabesque'? _____

3. Who worships in a 'mosque'? _____

4. The suffix '-esque' means resembling a style or characteristic. What does 'statuesque'

mean? _____

5. What would you do with a 'barque'? a) eat it; b) sail in it; c) listen to it. _____

Homophones

What are the different meanings of these two words?

cheque : _____

check : _____

Name............................. Date...................................

Wordsearch -el

```
p  i  r  c  e  l  f  l  a  n  n  e  l  k  m  i  n
c  x  p  a  r  c  e  l  s  h  r  i  s  e  o  c  q
h  d  o  n  w  r  s  a  h  d  e  l  w  n  d  s  u
a  r  s  c  o  u  n  d  r  e  l  q  i  n  e  b  a
n  o  v  e  l  e  i  r  i  m  a  r  v  e  l  a  r
n  k  e  l  u  l  v  e  v  j  b  u  e  l  n  r  r
e  i  t  r  a  v  e  l  e  e  k  l  a  d  r  e
l  s  h  o  v  e  l  d  l  w  l  t  u  n  n  e  l
t  e  b  u  e  l  g  e  l  e  c  e  n  c  e  l  b
o  l  m  o  r  s  e  l  t  l  u  l  j  u  w  e  l
```

Find each hidden word and write it on the line provided.
Use the LOOK, SAY, COVER, WRITE, CHECK method.

barrel	_____	novel	_____
cancel	_____	parcel	_____
channel	_____	quarrel	_____
flannel	_____	scoundrel	_____
jewel	_____	shrivel	_____
kennel	_____	shovel	_____
label	_____	snivel	_____
marvel	_____	swivel	_____
model	_____	travel	_____
morsel	_____	tunnel	_____

24a

Crossword

-el

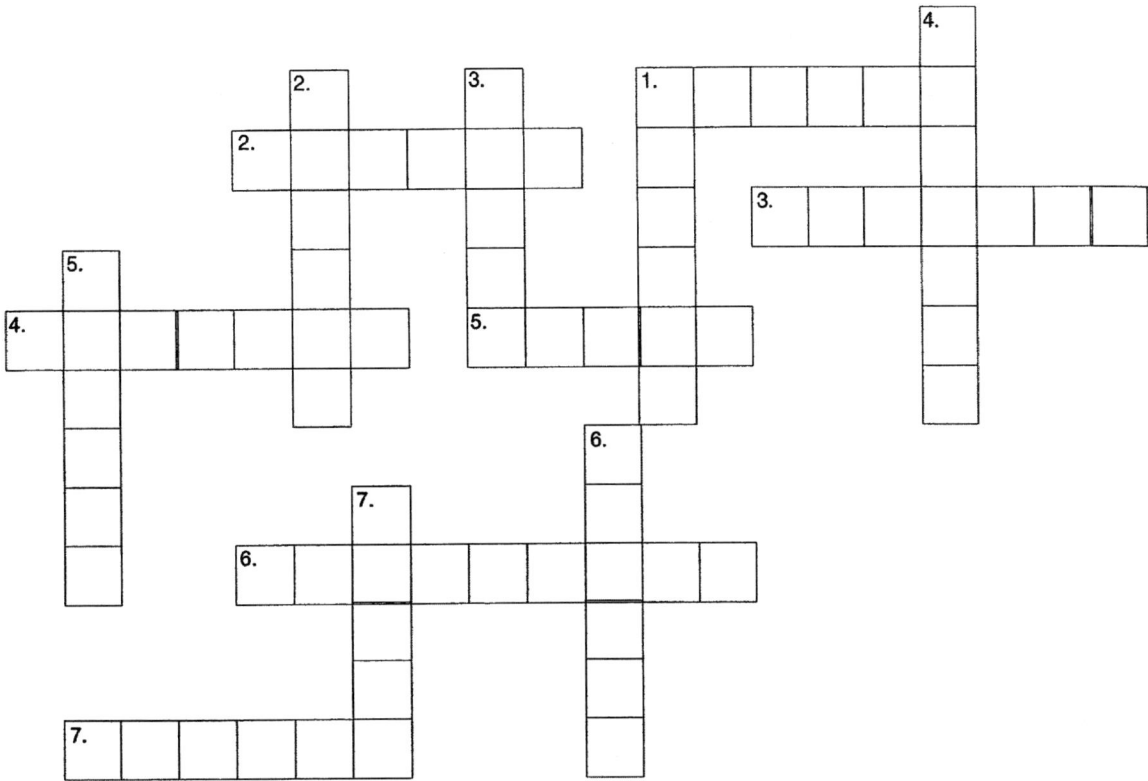

Across:

1. To feel astonishment and admiration.

2. To call off, or to cross out.

3. A groove.

4. To dry up; to shrink.

5. A piece of paper attached to something, showing what it is.

6. A dishonest or wicked person.

7. To turn round.

Down:

1. A small piece of food.

2: A wooden or metal cask.

3. A precious stone or gem.

4. A face-cloth used for washing.

5. A kind of spade.

6. A package, often wrapped in paper.

7. A long fiction story filling a whole book.

| channel | shovel | marvel | scoundrel | novel | flannel | label |
| shrivel | cancel | jewel | swivel | parcel | barrel | morsel |

Mixed Bag

-el

Change a Letter

Change one letter in each word to make a new word. A clue has been given for the new word. The first one has been done for you.

1.	kennel	(a herb used for flavouring)	_____fennel_____
2.	towel	(a, e, i, o, or u)	_____
3.	tunnel	(a metal chimney on a ship)	_____
4.	fuel	(a two-sided contest)	_____
5.	travel	(small stones)	_____
6.	snivel	(to turn round)	_____
7.	gruel	(brutal)	_____
8.	bevel	(to take great delight in something)	_____

Prefixes

You have been given the ending '-pel' which comes from Latin meaning 'drive'. Use the following prefixes to complete the words. Use your dictionary to help you if you are not sure.

com-   dis-   ex-   im-   pro-   re-

1.	to push forward and keep going by force	_ _ _ p e l
2.	to use irresistible force	_ _ _ p e l
3.	to cause to disappear	_ _ _ p e l
4.	to ward off	_ _ p e l
5.	to drive or urge forward	_ _ p e l
6.	to send away or force out	_ _ p e l

Homophones

Use your dictionary to find the different meanings of these homophones.

1.	kernel	_____
	colonel	_____
2.	duel	_____
	dual	_____
3.	navel	_____
	naval	_____
4.	mantel	_____
	mantle	_____
5.	counsel	_____
	council	_____
6.	mussel	_____
	muscle	_____

Wordsearch -et (ay)

```
o  d  u  v  e  t  o  c  h  a  l  e  t  w
b  u  c  a  b  o  u  q  u  e  t  x  p  o
u  v  a  l  c  u  v  b  d  s  t  e  b  e
f  l  b  e  a  r  r  i  c  o  c  h  e  t
f  e  a  t  b  n  q  d  l  r  r  c  r  p
e  t  r  e  n  i  u  e  t  b  o  f  e  a
t  f  e  t  k  q  e  t  r  e  q  e  t  r
i  m  t  g  o  u  r  m  e  t  u  t  c  q
c  b  a  l  l  e  t  e  t  h  e  t  h  u
s  a  c  h  e  t  q  u  o  e  t  e  s  e
t  l  l  e  t  o  a  c  r  o  c  h  e  t
```

Find each hidden word and write it on the line provided.
Use the LOOK, SAY, COVER, WRITE, CHECK method.

ballet	_____	duvet	_____
beret	_____	gourmet	_____
bidet	_____	parquet	_____
bouquet	_____	ricochet	_____
buffet	_____	sachet	_____
cabaret	_____	sorbet	_____
chalet	_____	tourniquet	_____
crochet	_____	valet	_____
croquet	_____		

Note: 'chalet' is pronounced 'shalay'; 'ricochet' - 'ricoshay'; 'crochet' - 'croshay';
        'sachet' - 'sashay'

Name............................. Date..............................

Crossword

-et (ay)

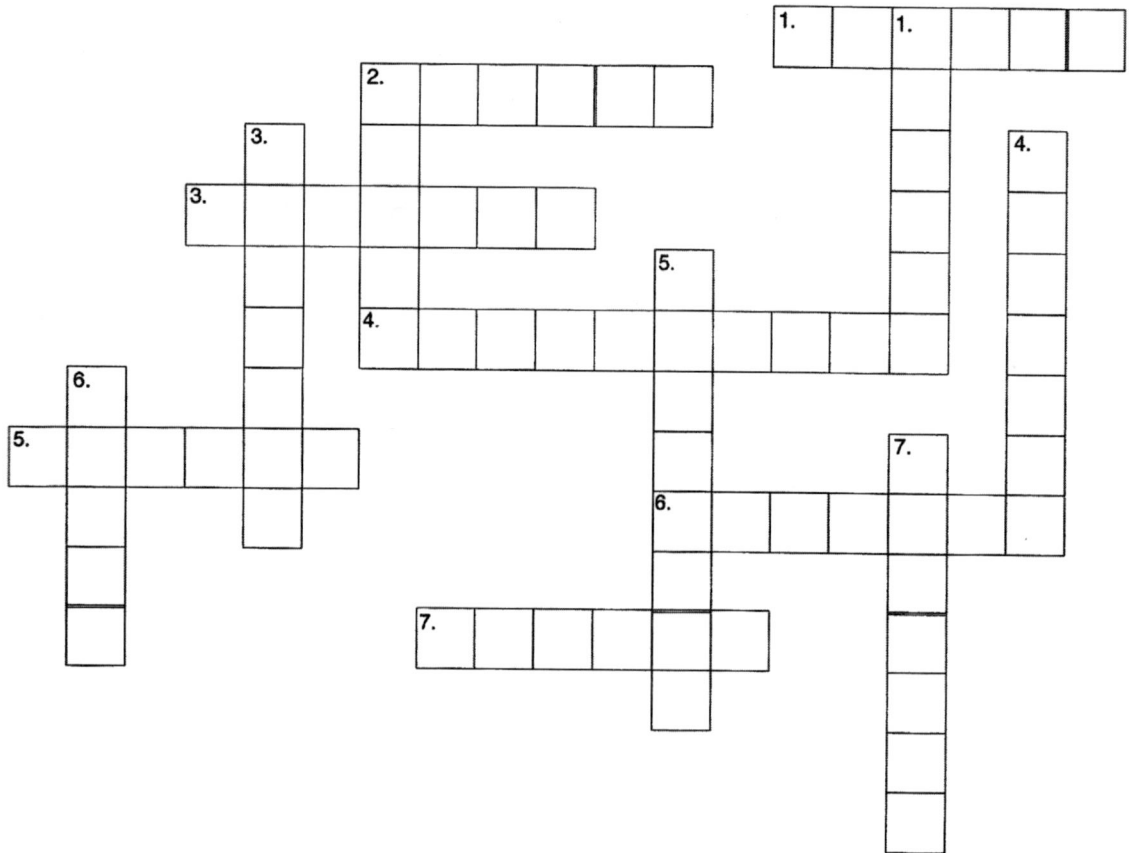

Across:

1. A small, sealed envelope or packet containing something, such as shampoo.

2. A story told in dance, set to music.

3. An expert on food and wine.

4. A device for stopping bleeding by applying pressure on the artery.

5. A meal where guests serve themselves.

6. Entertainment performed in a restaurant.

7. A sharp-tasting ice-water dessert, similar to ice-cream.

Down:

1. A small house or hut in a holiday camp or on a beach.

2. A round, flat cap without a peak.

3. A bunch of flowers.

4. Flooring made of wooden blocks laid in a pattern.

5. Rebounding off a surface; such as a bullet rebounding off a rock.

6 A thick, soft quilt for a bed.

7. A game played on a lawn, using mallets, hoops and a ball.

| bouquet | cabaret | duvet | parquet | sorbet | gourmet | beret |
| ballet | tourniquet | croquet | buffet | sachet | ricochet | chalet |

25b

Sound Activities - Extension Exercises

Name............................ Date...................................

Mixed Bag -et (ay)

Missing Words

Read through this passage and fill in the blanks with appropriate words from the following list.

bouquet   chalet   sorbet   gourmet   parquet   buffet   ballet

The shiny motor car was waiting to take the famous _____ dancer to a celebration

lunch. Upon her arrival, she was greeted warmly by the mayor, who presented her with a

beautiful _____ of flowers.

The lunch was magnificent and she congratulated the chef, who was a true _____,

on the superb _____ he had prepared for the guests. She sampled many of the

delicious foods. Unfortunately, she carelessly dropped a dish of lemon _____ on the

highly polished _____ floor. Feeling rather embarrassed, she made a hasty exit and

returned to her _____ at the foot of the mountains.

Most of the words from the above list come from the same language. Can you find out which
language? An etymological dictionary (one which gives the origins of words) will help you.

_____

Words Within Words

Solve the clue and write the word from the following list which has the answer inside it. The first
one has been done for you.

~~ballet~~   duvet   gourmet   cabaret   chalet   sorbet   buffet

1. used in some games   b a l l e t

2. beer   _ _ _ _ _ _

3. an animal doctor   _ _ _ _ _

4. unclothed   _ _ _ _ _ _ _

5. to polish with a soft cloth   _ _ _ _ _ _

6. belonging to us   _ _ _ _ _ _ _

7. a wager   _ _ _ _ _ _

Name.............................. Date....................................

Wordsearch

```
s  i  b  t  j  o  c  k  e  y  a  d  j  a  s  k
c  f  a  d  o  n  k  e  y  i  b  s  a  n  t  p
h  p  r  q  u  e  a  v  k  e  b  p  i  l  o  a
i  k  l  t  r  o  l  l  e  y  e  i  e  b  r  e
m  i  e  r  n  l  l  e  y  c  n  y  m  e  y
n  d  y  o  e  y  e  y  i  m  o  n  k  e  y  o
e  n  m  e  y  e  y  v  o  l  l  e  y  d  r  s
y  e  s  y  j  c  h  u  t  n  e  y  t  l  e  y
d  y  g  a  l  l  e  y  u  h  o  c  k  e  y  b
o  v  l  s  h  e  y  e  v  a  l  l  e  y  n  e
w  p  a  r  s  l  e  y  g  u  p  u  l  l  e  y
```

Find each hidden word and write it on the line provided.
Use the LOOK, SAY, COVER, WRITE, CHECK method.

abbey   _____   kidney   _____

alley   _____   medley   _____

barley   _____   monkey   _____

chimney   _____   parsley   _____

chutney   _____   pulley   _____

donkey   _____   spinney   _____

galley   _____   storey   _____

hockey   _____   trolley   _____

jockey   _____   valley   _____

journey   _____   volley   _____

Name.............................. Date..................................

Crossword

-ey (ē)

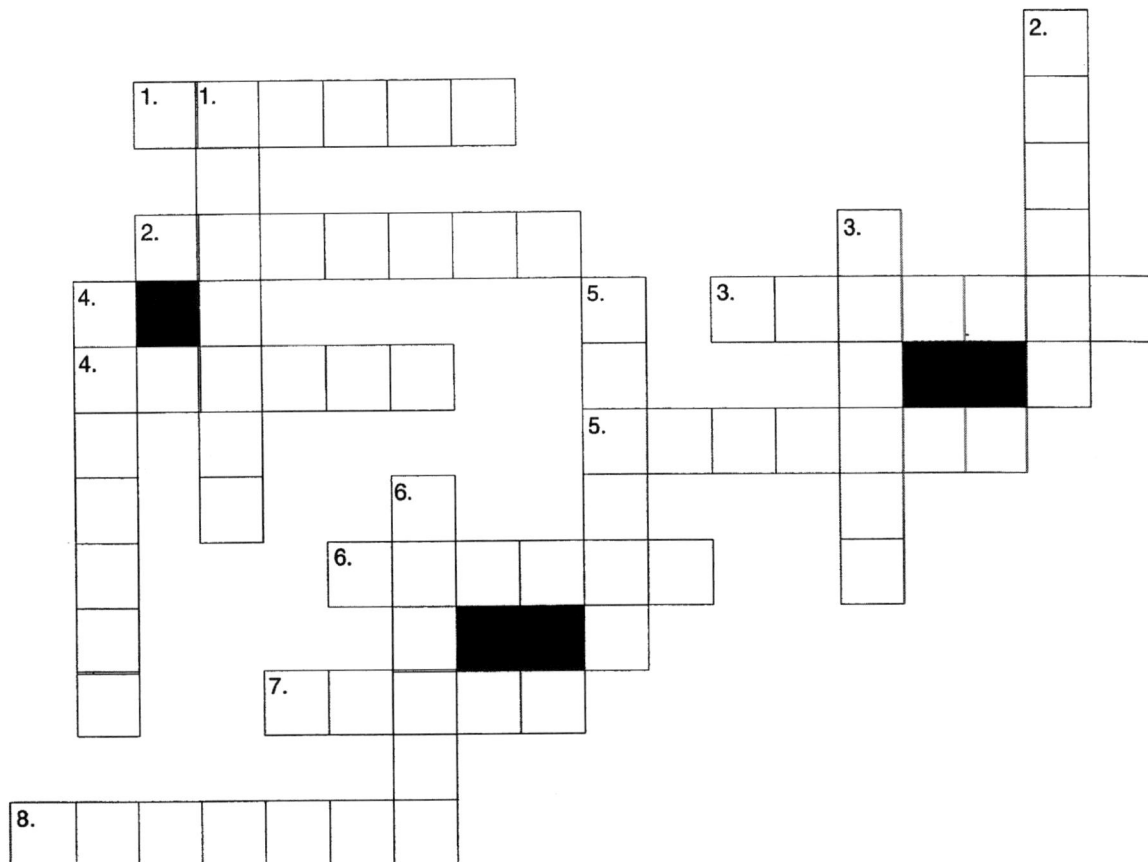

Across:

1. One of many floors of a building.

2. A trip.

3. A tube-like passage to carry away smoke.

4. A wheel with a grooved rim to take a rope, used for lifting things.

5. A strong-tasting mixture of fruit and spices, often eaten with meat.

6. A ship's kitchen.

7. A narrow passage or street.

8. A herb used in cooking.

Down:

1. A basket on wheels.

2. A team game played with curved sticks and a hard ball.

3. One of two organs in the body which remove waste matter from the blood.

4. A small wood.

5. A person who rides a racehorse.

6. An area of low land between hills.

pulley   jockey   parsley   trolley   storey   spinney   kidney
chutney   valley   alley   journey   galley   hockey   chimney

Name.............................. Date....................................

Mixed Bag   -ey (ē)

Odd One Out

Look at the first word and circle the word in the list which is the odd one out. Write the reason why on the line below. Use your dictionary to help you if you are not sure.

1. barley :   rye   carrot   wheat   oats

   Reason : _____

2. galley :   stern   deck   keel   beach

   Reason : _____

3. parsley :   thyme   sage   cabbage   rosemary

   Reason : _____

4. kidney :   heart   leg   lungs   brain

   Reason : _____

5. monkey :   ape   gorilla   dog   chimpanzee

   Reason : _____

6. spinney :   thicket   meadow   wood   copse

   Reason : _____

7. chimney :   roof   thatch   eaves   path

   Reason : _____

8. hockey :   cricket   swimming   squash   tennis

   Reason : _____

Change a Letter

Change one letter in each word to make a new word. Clues have been given to help you. The first one has been done for you.

1. monkey   (animal Mary rode into Bethlehem)   _____donkey_____

2. galley   (low area between hills)   _____

3. hockey   (person who rides a racehorse)   _____

4. kidney   (a boy's name)   _____

5. parsley   (a swirling pattern on fabric)   _____

6. money   (bees make it)   _____

7. Jersey   (an English river)   _____

8. Cockney   (an English artist born in 1937)   _____

Islands Around Britain

1. an island off north-west Wales   A _ _ _ _ _ _ _

2. the second largest of the Channel Islands   G _ _ _ _ _ _ _

3. a group of islands off the north-east tip of Scotland O _ _ _ _ _ _

26c

Sound Activities - Extension Exercises

Name............................... Date...................................

Wordsearch

```
t  o  a  g  e  n  d  a  a  d  i  l  e  m  m  a
i  p  u  t  p  u  m  b  r  e  l  l  a  s  a  m
v  e  s  r  e  t  h  m  o  c  o  t  s  t  a  p
a  l  p  a  n  o  r  a  m  a  r  e  n  a  p  o
n  a  e  u  i  r  e  c  a  n  c  o  i  m  a  p
i  d  n  m  n  s  p  a  l  o  h  x  m  i  s  e
l  r  u  a  s  a  l  c  a  m  e  r  a  n  a  r
l  a  s  t  u  r  i  n  a  e  s  a  g  a  n  a
a  m  p  u  l  a  c  o  l  r  t  r  a  m  a  n
n  a  t  r  a  b  a  l  l  e  r  i  n  a  g  t
m  e  x  t  r  a  p  r  a  v  a  m  i  c  h  o
```

Find each hidden word and write it on the line provided.
Use the LOOK, SAY, COVER, WRITE, CHECK method.

agenda	_____	orchestra	_____
arena	_____	panorama	_____
aroma	_____	peninsula	_____
ballerina	_____	replica	_____
camera	_____	saga	_____
dilemma	_____	stamina	_____
drama	_____	trauma	_____
extra	_____	umbrella	_____
opera	_____	vanilla	_____

Name............................. Date.................................

Crossword

-a

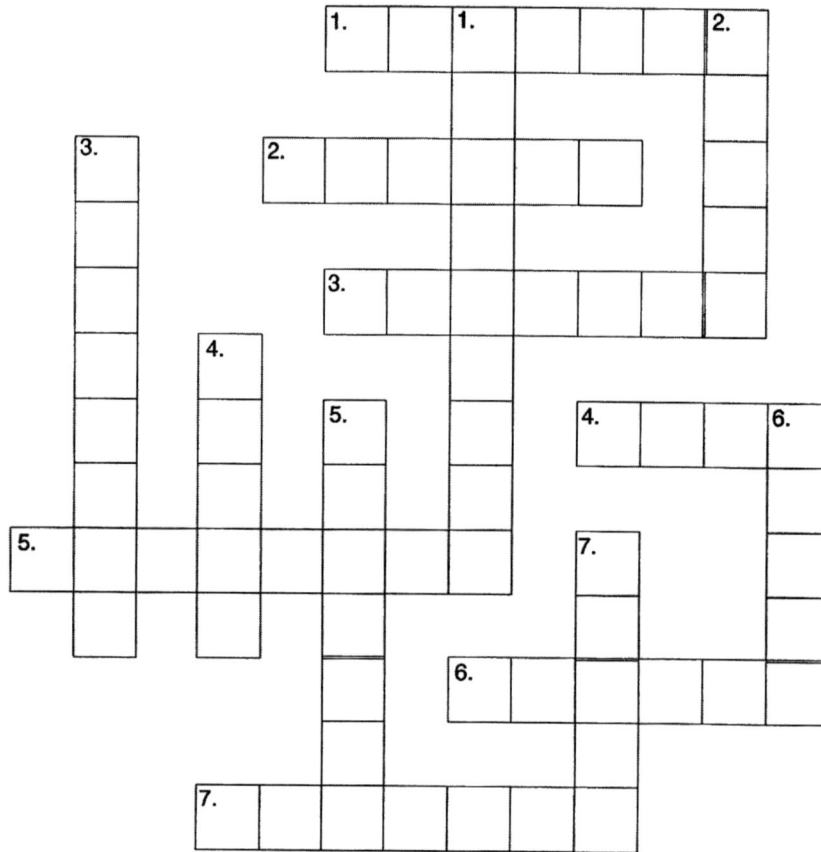

Across:

1. An exact copy.

2. Items of business to be discussed at a meeting.

3. A flavour, particularly of ice-cream.

4. A long story of heroic achievement; a long involved story.

5. A folding device carried as protection against rain.

6. A state of shock following an extremely stressful event.

7. The ability to endure pain or hard effort over a long period of time.

Down:

1. An area of land jutting out into the sea, almost surrounded by water.

2. The place where a sports event takes place.

3. A wide view of scenery.

4. More than usual.

5. A difficult situation forcing someone to make a choice between two things.

6. A pleasant smell of food.

7. The performance of a play.

vanilla	panorama	peninsula	saga	drama	umbrella	agenda
extra	dilemma	trauma	stamina	aroma	arena	replica

Sound Activities - Extension Exercises

Name.............................. Date..................................

Mixed Bag   -a

Odd One Out

Circle the odd word out and then write the reason why.

1. gorilla   panda   koala   aroma   zebra   puma

   Reason : _____

2. Ghana   Argentina   Africa   Canada   China

   Reason : _____

3. harmonica   tuba   viola   ocarina   villa

   Reason : _____

4. Argentina   Bolivia   China   Venezuela   Colombia

   Reason : _____

5. mamba   cobra   boa   tarantula   anaconda

   Reason : _____

6. satsuma   tuna   papaya   sultana   banana

   Reason : _____

7. Sheila   Veronica   Fiona   Paula   Kenya   Anna

   Reason : _____

8. opera   orchestra   sonata   tombola   viola

   Reason : _____

9. Ottawa   Canberra   Vienna   Canada   Lima

   Reason : _____

Countries and Capitals

Match the country with its capital city. If you are not sure, use an atlas to help you. The first one has been done for you.

Country	Capital City
1. Canada	Colombo
2. Sri Lanka	Nairobi
3. Venezuela	Beijing
4. Argentina	Ottawa
5. China	Havana
6. Libya	Caracus
7. Nicaragua	Accra
8. Kenya	Buenos Aires
9. Cuba	Managua
10. Ghana	Tripoli

Wordsearch   -i (ē)

```
s  m  b  s  p  a  g  h  e  t  t  i  j  k  i  h  o
a  u  a  c  r  k  r  i  x  b  o  r  a  h  g  a  r
r  e  k  a  a  s  a  f  a  r  i  c  u  a  r  s  i
f  s  i  m  i  u  f  s  l  o  d  i  z  k  i  c  g
i  l  s  p  k  l  f  j  a  c  u  z  z  i  s  i  a
b  i  k  i  n  i  i  t  o  c  a  m  i  c  a  t  m
a  j  i  n  i  f  t  i  p  o  t  p  o  u  r  r  i
s  c  h  i  l  l  i  m  i  l  i  d  e  l  i  o  s
i  e  c  o  n  f  e  t  t  i  v  s  t  a  x  i  n
```

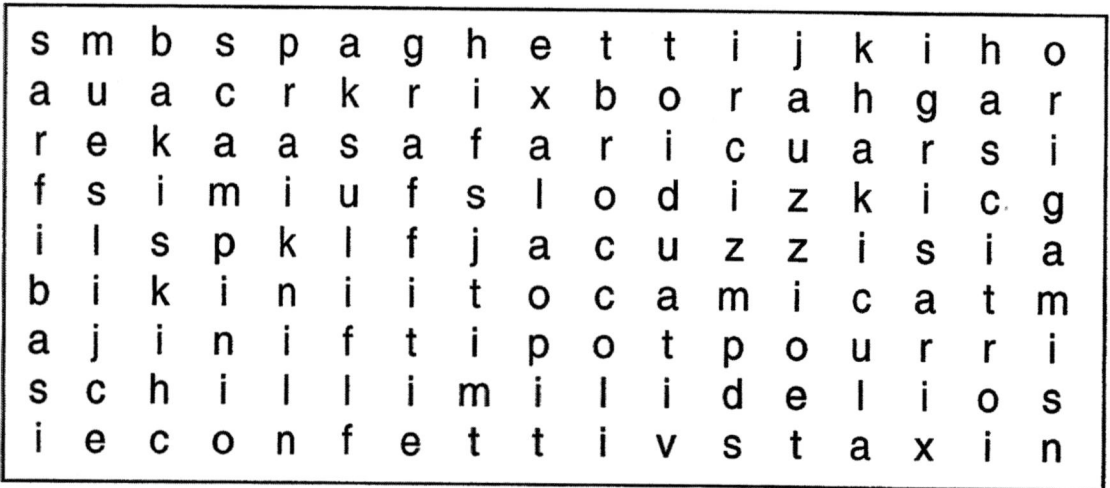

Find each hidden word and write it on the line provided.
Use the LOOK, SAY, COVER, WRITE, CHECK method.

bikini	_____	origami	_____
broccoli	_____	pot-pourri	_____
chilli	_____	safari	_____
confetti	_____	sari	_____
graffiti	_____	scampi	_____
jacuzzi	_____	ski	_____
khaki	_____	spaghetti	_____
muesli	_____	taxi	_____

Sound Activities - Extension Exercises

Name............................... Date...................................

Crossword

-i (ē)

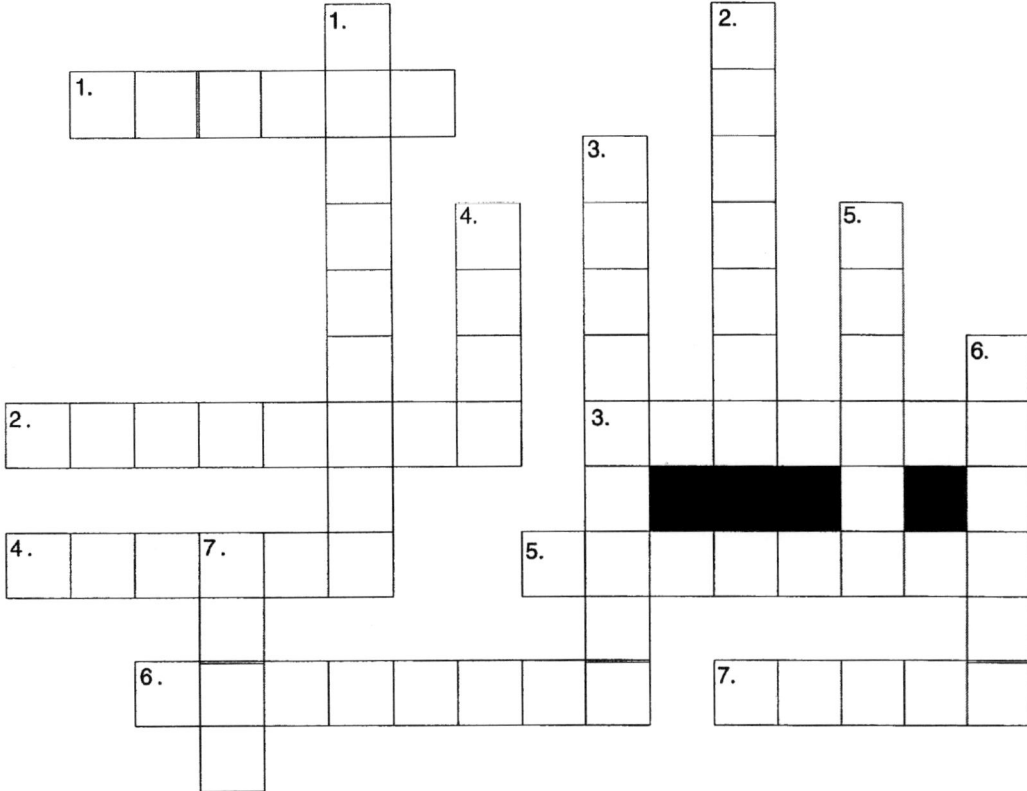

Across:

1. Large prawns, breaded and fried.

2. Small pieces of coloured paper thrown over the bride and bridegroom by wedding guests.

3. Folded paper to make animals or other shapes.

4. A breakfast cereal of crushed cereals, nuts and dried fruit.

5. Writing and drawings done on the walls of buildings.

6. A green vegetable, similar to a cauliflower.

7. A dull brownish-yellow colour.

Down:

1. Pasta in long, thin strands.

2. A bath with swirling water.

3. A mixture of dried petals, perfumed to give a pleasant fragrance.

4. A car and driver you can hire to take you somewhere.

5. An expedition to see animals in the wild.

6. A woman's two-piece bathing suit.

7. A long length of cloth worn as a dress.

confetti   jacuzzi   bikini   muesli   spaghetti   graffiti   pot-pourri
sari   scampi   safari   origami   broccoli   taxi   khaki

Mixed Bag

-i (ē)

Some General Knowledge Questions

Use a dictionary or encyclopedia to help you if you are not sure of the answers. Underline the word ending in 'i' in each question before answering it.

1. In which state of America is Miami? _____

2. New Delhi is the capital city of which country? _____

3. A corgi is a breed of which animal? _____

4. The art of folding paper, called Origami, originated in which country?_____

5. Helsinki is the capital city of which country? _____

6. In which ocean will you find the islands of Fiji? _____

7. A kiwi is a flightless bird, but which country does it come from? _____

8. Is a sari worn by a male or a female? _____

Food From Around the World

Draw a line to connect the food to the country it comes from. The first one has been done for you.

Food	Country
1. chilli con carne	Japan
2. chapati	Italy
3. muesli	Mexico
4. sushi	Switzerland
5. spaghetti	India

A Long Name For A Long River

This is one of the longest rivers in North America - it has 11 letters, but only 4 different ones. The only vowel is 'i' and has been filled in for you. Can you complete the name?

_ i _ _ i _ _ i _ _ i

Anagrams

Rearrange the letters of these anagrams to make the following words.

SAFARI   CONFETTI   BROCCOLI   GRAFFITI   SPAGHETTI   POT-POURRI

1. EIGHT TAPS _____   4. TO INFECT _____

2. COOL CRIB _____   5. RIP UP ROOT _____

3. IS AFAR _____   6. FAIR GIFT _____

Name............................. Date.................................

Wordsearch -o (ō)

```
o  f  l  a  m  i  n  g  o  t  z  e  r  o  t  i
m  l  s  o  l  l  t  u  c  q  u  x  t  r  z  b
e  b  o  m  i  m  o  s  q  u  i  t  o  i  e  l
m  r  l  f  n  o  r  t  u  d  n  p  m  o  c  o
e  v  o  l  c  a  n  o  p  i  f  o  a  n  h  s
n  o  s  p  o  t  a  t  o  z  e  t  t  m  o  t
t  e  l  o  g  a  d  o  k  e  r  a  o  o  f  a
o  t  c  o  n  s  o  r  r  a  n  o  v  t  o  m
c  h  u  f  i  a  s  c  o  r  o  t  w  t  h  a
m  o  q  u  t  o  v  a  m  c  a  r  g  o  i  t
o  l  b  i  o  s  t  r  o  g  l  a  o  v  h  o
```

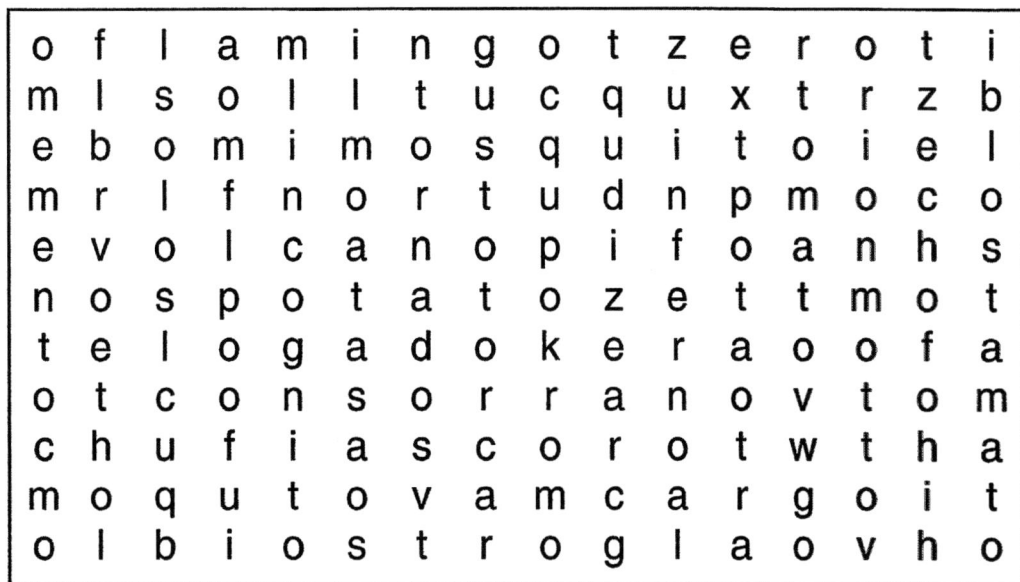

Find each hidden word and write it on the line provided.
Use the LOOK, SAY, COVER, WRITE, CHECK method.

cargo _____   mosquito _____

echo _____   motto _____

fiasco _____   potato _____

flamingo _____   solo _____

gusto _____   tomato _____

incognito _____   tornado _____

inferno _____   volcano _____

memento _____   zero _____

Name............................... Date.....................................

Crossword

-o (ō)

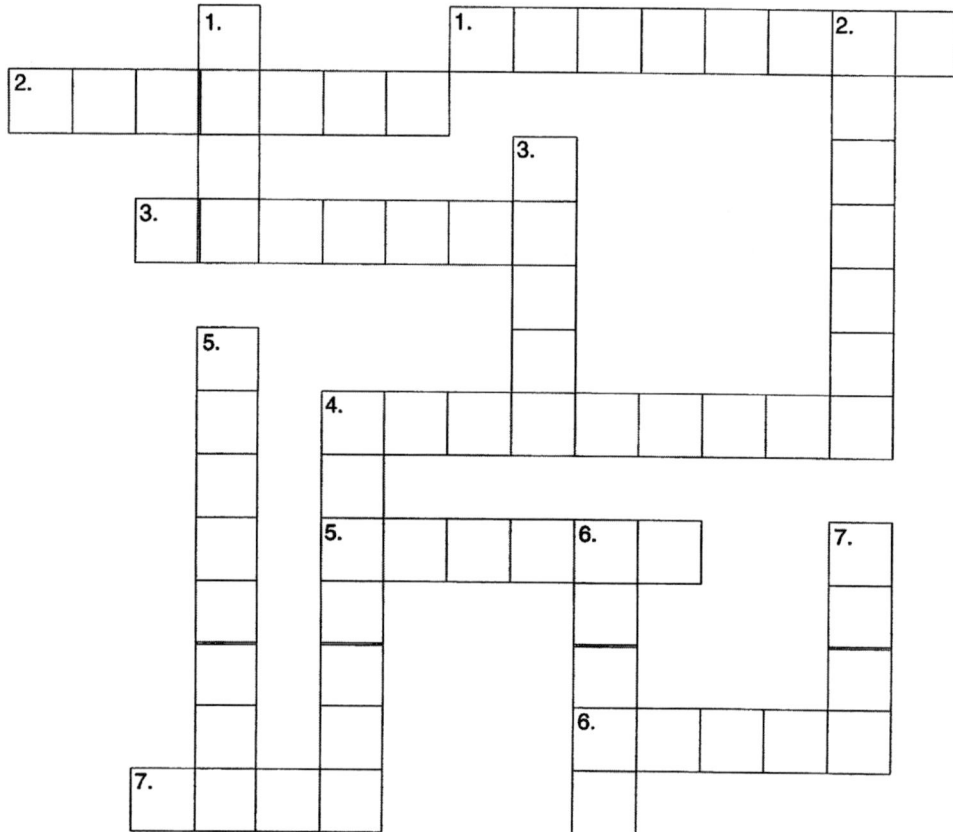

Across:

1. A biting insect.

2. A keepsake; a reminder.

3. A mountain which can erupt.

4. In disguise in order to keep identity hidden.

5. A humiliating and complete failure.

6. Great enjoyment in doing something.

7. A piece of music played by one person.

Down:

1. Nothing; nought.

2. A violent storm or whirlwind.

3. A saying adopted as a rule of conduct.

4. A raging, uncontrollable fire.

5. A pink bird with a long neck and long legs.

6. A ship's load.

7. A repetition of a sound caused by sound waves being reflected.

tornado	inferno	gusto	memento	zero	flamingo	echo
solo	volcano	mosquito	motto	incognito	fiasco	cargo

29b

Name........................... Date.................................

Mixed Bag

-o (ō)

Countries, Capital Cities and Continents

What is the capital city of each of these countries and in which continent is each to be found?
Use an atlas to help you.

		Capital City	Continent
1.	Norway		
2.	Egypt		
3.	Japan		
4.	Sri Lanka		
5.	Ecuador		

Odd One Out

Circle the odd word out and then write the reason why.

1. tomato   sago   vertigo   potato

    Reason : _____

2. piano   banjo   piccolo   mango   cello

    Reason : _____

3. flamingo   cargo   buffalo   mosquito   dingo

    Reason : _____

4. soprano   maestro   concerto   torso   crescendo

    Reason : _____

What Do These Words Have In Common?

trio   triplet   triple   treble   triplicate   trilogy

_____

Synonyms

From the words below, find 10 pairs of words which have similar meanings. If you are not sure,
use your dictionary or thesaurus to help you.

cargo   inferno   unaccompanied   nought   disguised   buffalo   hero
blaze   motto   keepsake   zero   incognito   gusto   champion   freight
           slogan   memento   enthusiasm   bison   solo

1. _____   _____   6. _____   _____

2. _____   _____   7. _____   _____

3. _____   _____   8. _____   _____

4. _____   _____   9. _____   _____

5. _____   _____   10. _____   _____

Sound Activities - Extension Exercises

Wordsearch

-ē, -ī and -ū

```
r  i  m  p  r  o  m  p  t  u  s  m  u  n  g
a  t  e  c  a  g  k  u  r  u  r  a  n  a  u
b  g  n  o  b  a  l  i  b  i  e  g  i  n  r
e  m  u  i  b  i  c  p  h  e  c  i  s  e  u
p  n  t  s  i  m  i  l  e  p  i  t  o  m  e
a  p  o  s  t  r  o  p  h  e  p  e  m  o  t
k  h  a  i  k  u  g  b  b  i  e  b  e  n  u
u  i  m  c  a  t  a  s  t  r  o  p  h  e  r
```

**Find each hidden word and write it on the line provided.
Use the LOOK, SAY, COVER, WRITE, CHECK method.**

anemone _____   alibi _____

apostrophe _____   Magi _____

catastrophe _____   rabbi _____

epitome _____

recipe _____   emu _____

simile _____   guru _____

haiku _____

impromptu _____

menu _____

30a

Name............................. Date..................................

Crossword $-\bar{e}$, $-\bar{i}$ and $-\bar{u}$

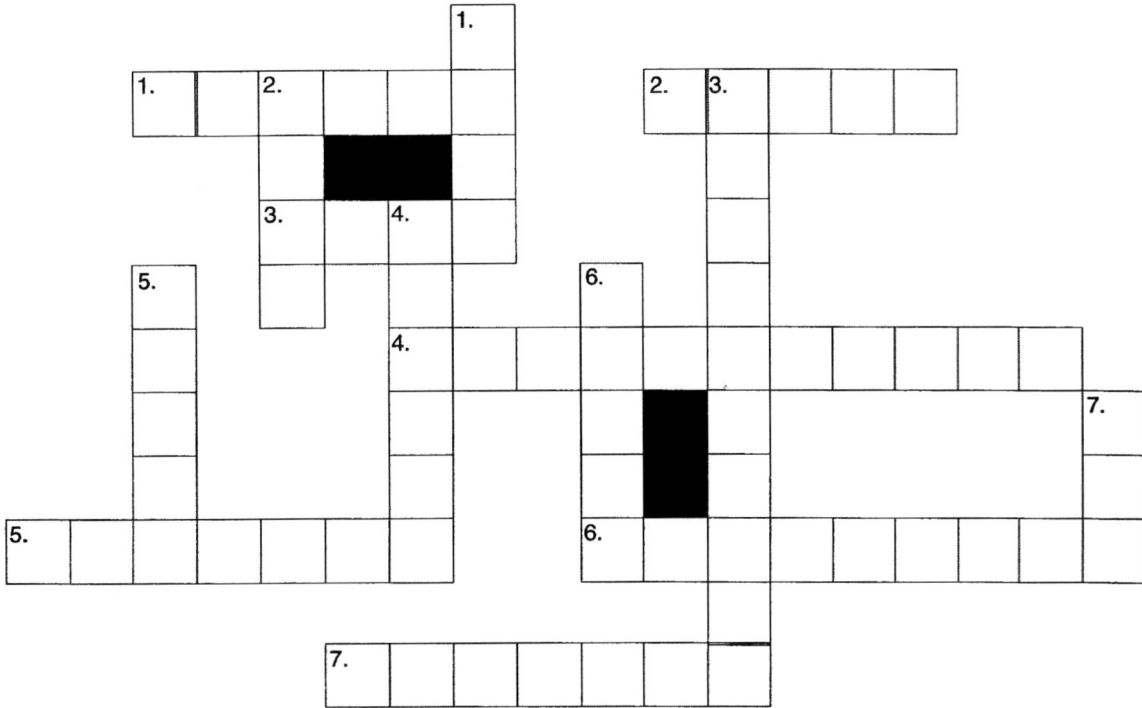

Across:

1. A phrase which makes a comparison - e.g. as cold as ice.

2. A Japanese poem of 3 lines and 17 syllables.

3. A Hindu spiritual teacher.

4. A sudden, great disaster.

5. The perfect example of something.

6. Unrehearsed.

7. A kind of flower; also a sea creature with tentacles resembling a flower.

Down:

1. A list of food offered in a restaurant.

2. The wise men who brought Jesus gifts at his birth.

3. A form of punctuation which indicates possession or shortening of words.

4. Ingredients and method for preparing and cooking food.

5. Evidence that someone accused of a crime was somewhere else at the time.

6. A Jewish religious leader.

7. A flightless bird of Australia.

| alibi | catastrophe | rabbi | emu | epitome | recipe | haiku | simile |
| apostrophe | Magi | anemone | | menu | impromptu | | guru |

30b

Sound Activities - Extension Exercises

Mixed Bag

-ē, -ī and -ū

Words Within Words

Solve the clue and write the word from the following list which has the answer inside it. The first one has been done for you.

anemone   apostrophe   catastrophe   epitome   simile   impromptu   ~~menu~~

1. plural of man   <u>m</u> <u>e</u> <u>n</u> <u>u</u>

2. punctual   _ _ _ _ _ _ _ _ _

3. object pronoun form of I   _ _ _ _ _ _ _

4. a furry domestic animal   _ _ _ _ _ _ _ _ _ _

5. the first number   _ _ _ _ _ _ _

6. a measure of distance   _ _ _ _ _

7. a piece of wood or metal set in the ground   _ _ _ _ _ _ _ _

Plurals

Some singular nouns (especially from Latin) have endings which change to 'i' (long vowel sound) when they are in plural form.

For example: **radius** (a line from the centre to the circumference of a circle) becomes **radii** when in the plural form.

Write the plural form of each of these singular words ending in '-us'. Look up the word in your dictionary if you are not sure of its meaning.

	Singular Form	**Plural Form**
1.	fungus	_____
2.	stimulus	_____
3.	cactus	_____
4.	nucleus	_____
5.	thesaurus	_____

Synonyms

From the words below, find 10 pairs of words which have similar meanings. If you are not sure, use your dictionary or thesaurus to help you.

catastrophe   recipe   teacher   epitome   comparison   disaster   guru
essence   formula   alibi   spontaneous   simile   excuse   impromptu

1. _____   _____   5. _____   _____

2. _____   _____   6. _____   _____

3. _____   _____   7. _____   _____

4. _____   _____

30c

Name............................   Date....................................

Wordsearch   -tial

```
n  p  a  p  a  r  t  i  a  l  s  p  a  t  i  a  l  c
e  r  r  a  n  p  o  t  i  a  l  a  s  x  d  s  m  r
s  e  e  l  p  u  r  n  s  t  u  r  u  m  i  t  a  e
s  f  s  a  l  m  r  i  t  i  a  l  b  o  t  i  r  d
e  e  i  t  i  b  e  l  r  o  c  i  s  s  i  a  t  e
n  r  d  i  c  o  n  f  i  d  e  n  t  i  a  l  i  n
t  e  e  a  t  f  t  i  a  l  t  i  a  l  l  g  a  t
i  n  n  l  a  i  n  f  l  u  e  n  t  i  a  l  l  i
a  t  t  k  l  d  a  t  a  i  n  i  t  i  a  l  u  a
l  i  i  t  i  a  l  e  b  a  r  t  i  a  l  p  t  l
c  a  a  i  m  p  a  r  t  i  a  l  a  p  i  l  i  s
u  l  l  s  e  q  u  e  n  t  i  a  l  a  t  i  a  l
s  p  o  t  e  n  t  i  a  l  i  m  u  t  i  a  l  s
```

Find each hidden word and write it on the line provided.
Use the LOOK, SAY, COVER, WRITE, CHECK method.

confidential	_____	partial	_____
credentials	_____	potential	_____
essential	_____	preferential	_____
impartial	_____	residential	_____
influential	_____	sequential	_____
initial	_____	spatial	_____
martial	_____	substantial	_____
palatial	_____	torrential	_____

31a

Name.............................. Date..................................

Crossword

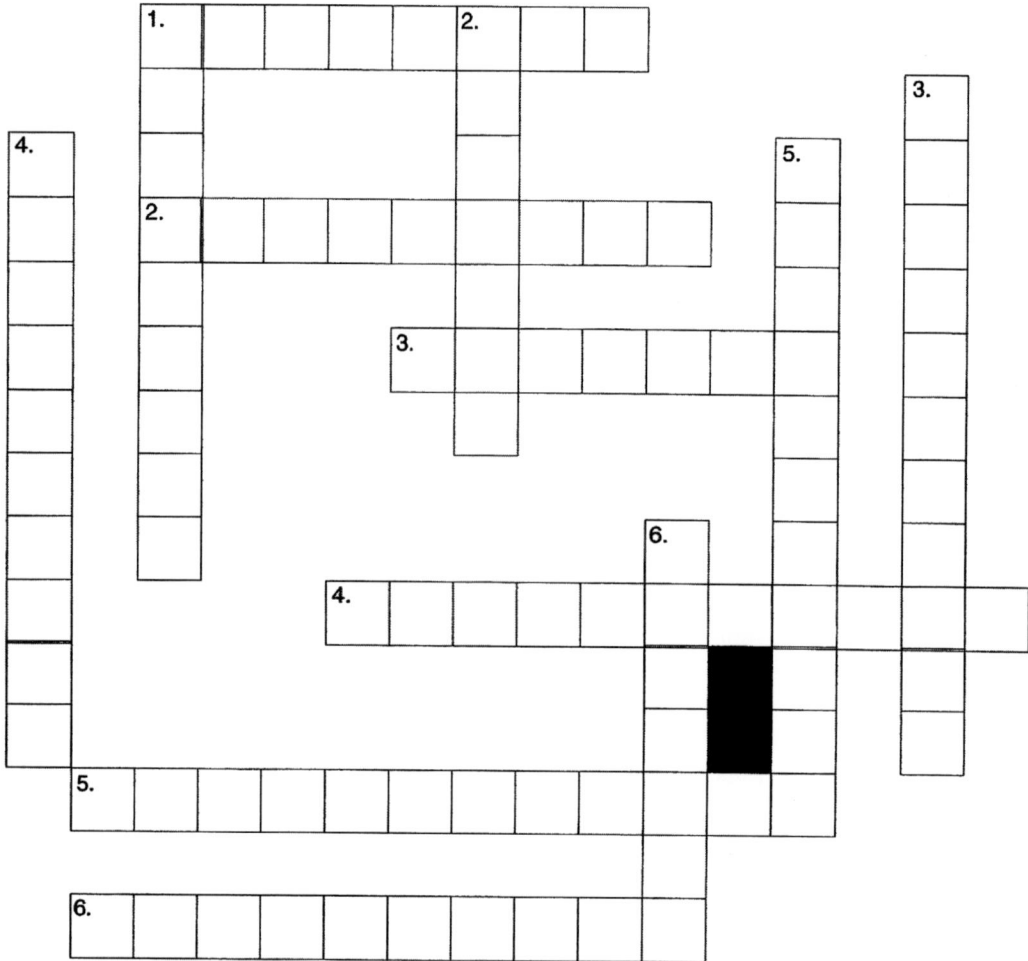

Across:

1. Splendid; like a palace.

2. Absolutely necessary.

3. Not complete; forming only a part of something.

4. Large or important.

5. To be kept secret.

6. Forming a sequence.

Down:

1. Capable of happening or doing something useful in the future.

2. The first letter of a name.

3. Letter or letters of recommendation; evidence of achievements.

4. Rapidly and violently flowing.

5. Having great influence.

6. To do with war or fighting.

essential   torrential   martial   influential   palatial   initial
potential   sequential   credentials   substantial   partial   confidential

31b

Name................................ Date..................................

Mixed Bag   -tial

Anagrams

Rearrange the letters of these anagrams to make the following words.

RESIDENTIAL   CONFIDENTIAL   INITIAL   TORRENTIAL   PREFERENTIAL
PARTIAL   CREDENTIALS   SUBSTANTIAL   SPATIAL   POTENTIAL   ESSENTIAL

1. ALIEN SETS _____   7. ROTTEN RAIL _____

2. I NAIL IT _____   8. AIRLINES TED _____

3. TRAIL PA _____   9. ATLANTIS BUS _____

4. INFANTILE COD _____   10. PLANET TIO _____

5. TAP LISA _____   11. FLEE TERRAPIN _____

6. SILENCED RAT_____

Nouns, Verbs and Adjectives

Write the noun, verb or adjective in the correct column. If you are not sure, use your dictionary.

	Noun	Verb	Adjective
1.	confidence		
2.		prefer	
3.			sequential
4.	influence		
5.			residential

Missing Words
Choose the correct word from the following list to complete these sentences.

substantial   impartial   partial   preferential   confidential   palatial

1. Nobody must know about this information - it must be kept strictly _____.

2. His judgement on the matter is totally fair and _____.

3. The actor owns a _____ house in the country.

4. If I am to be fair to you all, I cannot give anyone _____ treatment.

5. She had been left a _____ amount of money in her uncle's will.

6. My father is very _____ to roast turkey with lots of vegetables.

TIP:	The ending '-tial' is pronounced 'shal', but don't be tempted to spell it with 'sh'. The only word ending with the spelling 'shal' is 'marshal'.

31c

Wordsearch

-cial

```
p  e  s  p  e  c  i  s  u  p  e  r  f  i  c  i  a  l
r  b  o  r  s  o  f  f  i  c  i  a  l  p  r  o  n  s
o  e  c  r  e  c  i  a  l  u  t  r  u  c  i  a  l  p
v  n  i  a  b  e  n  e  f  i  s  t  r  u  c  b  l  e
i  e  a  d  e  s  a  c  r  i  f  i  c  i  a  l  a  c
n  v  l  i  n  u  n  c  o  g  o  f  a  c  i  a  l  i
c  o  m  m  e  r  c  i  a  l  c  i  a  l  l  c  s  a
i  c  a  f  c  i  a  l  a  i  c  r  u  c  i  a  l
a  i  s  i  c  a  l  c  c  a  i  l  r  r  a  h  c
l  a  p  a  c  i  l  h  u  i  l  a  b  c  o  l  c  i
d  l  r  l  i  a  n  e  s  a  c  l  g  i  s  t  i  a
o  s  c  i  a  l  a  m  u  l  t  i  r  a  c  i  a  l
s  e  n  p  l  s  u  p  e  r  c  i  a  l  k  r  l  o
```

Find each hidden word and write it on the line provided.
Use the LOOK, SAY, COVER, WRITE, CHECK method.

artificial	_____	multiracial	_____
beneficial	_____	official	_____
commercial	_____	provincial	_____
crucial	_____	sacrificial	_____
facial	_____	social	_____
financial	_____	special	_____
glacial	_____	superficial	_____

Sound Activities - Extension Exercises

Name............................ Date.................................

Crossword

-cial

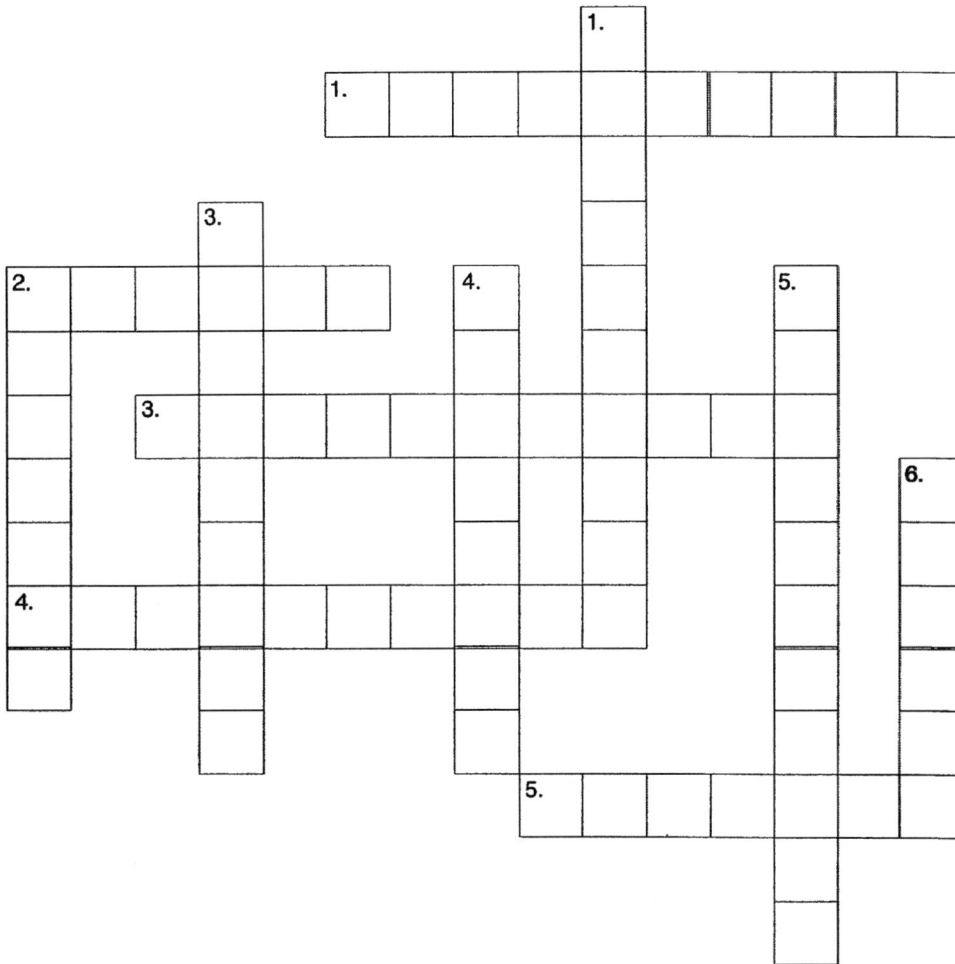

Across:

1. An advertisement, particularly on the television.

2. Living in groups or societies; concerned with society.

3. To do with offering something to a god.

4. Man-made, not natural.

5. Of the utmost importance.

Down:

1. Useful; advantageous.

2. Unusual; of a rare kind.

3. To do with money matters.

4. Done or said with authority.

5. Of many races or peoples.

6. To do with the face.

artificial   official   multiracial   commercial   special
facial   sacrificial   financial   crucial   beneficial   social

Sound Activities - Extension Exercises

Mixed Bag
-cial

Find the Mystery Word

The following words fit the squares below. Some letters have been given to help you. When you have completed the boxes, a mystery word will be revealed.

official   artificial   financial   facial   glacial   social   multiracial

1.				l			
2.		i		c			
3.		i	a				
4.	f						
5.	o						
6.			n				
7.	c						

Your answer is extremely important!_____

Nouns and Adjectives

Complete these columns with either the noun or the adjective. Use your dictionary to help you if you are not sure.

	Noun	Adjective
1.	face	
2.		glacial
3.	speciality	
4.		racial
5.		beneficial
6.	sacrifice	
7.	finance	
8.		provincial

Anagrams

Rearrange the letters of these anagrams to make some adjectives from above.

1. SLAP ICE   _____

2. I FLEE CABIN _____

3. FINAL INCA _____

4. RIP VAN CLIO _____

> **TIP:** Remember - although '-cial' is pronounced 'shal', 'marshal' is the only word spelt this way.

Wordsearch

-eon

```
f  l  u  e  o  n  p  i  d  e  o  n  g  t  o
c  u  f  p  i  g  e  o  n  d  r  i  o  r  s
h  n  b  l  u  n  d  g  i  e  o  n  l  u  u
a  g  l  s  c  r  e  o  n  t  r  e  u  n  r
m  h  u  g  o  s  t  u  r  g  e  o  n  d  g
e  e  d  e  s  c  h  e  v  a  h  n  c  g  e
l  o  g  o  l  l  e  o  n  l  g  s  h  e  o
e  n  e  n  d  e  o  n  p  l  e  a  e  o  n
o  t  o  t  r  u  n  c  h  e  o  n  o  m  o
n  m  n  c  h  a  m  l  e  o  n  b  n  e  e
c  o  n  d  u  n  g  e  o  n  d  m  e  o  n
```

Find each hidden word and write it on the line provided.
Use the LOOK, SAY, COVER, WRITE, CHECK method.

bludgeon	_____	neon	_____
chameleon	_____	pigeon	_____
dungeon	_____	sturgeon	_____
galleon	_____	surgeon	_____
luncheon	_____	truncheon	_____

Crossword

-eon

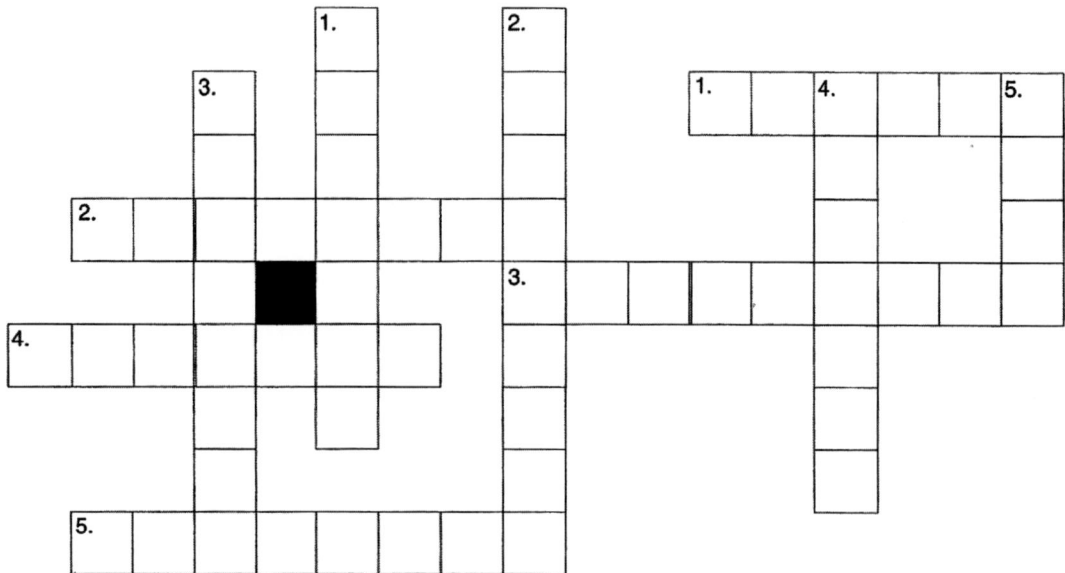

Across:

1. A bird.

2. A fish from which caviar is obtained.

3. A lizard which can change its colour to blend in with its surroundings.

4. A doctor who performs operations.

5. A more formal word for the midday meal.

Down:

1. An underground cell for prisoners.

2. A short, thick stick carried by policemen as a weapon.

3. To strike someone repeatedly with a short, thick club.

4. A large 16th or 17th century Spanish sailing ship.

5. A gas which glows when electricity passes through it, used for street lights and advertising signs.

| chameleon | truncheon | luncheon | galleon | surgeon |
| neon | bludgeon | pigeon | dungeon | sturgeon |

33b

Mixed Bag

-eon

Something Fishy's Going On Here!

You have been given the word sturgeon. Can you build these words around it?

dungeon   truncheon   neon   bludgeon   surgeon
luncheon   chameleon   burgeon

1. s
2. t
3. u
4. r
5. g
6. e
7. o
8. n

Definitions

Use your dictionary to find the meaning of each of these words.

1.   burgeon _____

2.   curmudgeon _____

3.   escutcheon _____

Anagrams

Rearrange the letters of these anagrams to make the following words.

CHAMELEON   DUNGEON   BLUDGEON   SURGEON   GALLEON   PIGEON

1.   ALL GONE _____   4.   CLEAN HOME _____

2.   BOUND LEG _____   5.   ONE PIG _____

3.   NUDGE ON _____   6.   GO NURSE _____

Idioms

What is meant by each of these expressions?

1.   put the cat among the pigeons - to make enemies
                                     - to try to get on with people
                                     - to cause trouble

2.   something is your pigeon   - someone has found a bird
                                     - you have to deal with a situation
                                     - you have a mess to clear up

33c

Wordsearch

-gue

```
o  d  a  p  l  a  g  u  e  t  a  c  h  i  w  i
p  i  c  e  a  g  u  e  l  l  e  a  g  u  e  n
l  a  i  p  r  o  l  o  g  u  e  t  t  v  l  t
a  l  p  i  l  v  i  g  u  e  a  a  r  o  g  r
c  o  l  l  e  a  g  u  e  p  o  l  o  g  u  i
o  g  r  o  m  g  m  o  n  o  l  o  g  u  e  g
g  u  g  g  e  u  s  t  o  l  u  g  u  e  x  u
u  e  u  u  f  e  f  a  t  i  g  u  e  t  g  e
e  b  e  e  a  n  a  l  o  g  u  e  n  d  u  k
s  y  n  a  g  o  g  u  e  t  o  n  g  u  e  n
```

Find each hidden word and write it on the line provided.
Use the LOOK, SAY, COVER, WRITE, CHECK method.

analogue   _____   monologue   _____

catalogue   _____   plague   _____

colleague   _____   prologue   _____

dialogue   _____   rogue   _____

epilogue   _____   synagogue   _____

fatigue   _____   tongue   _____

intrigue   _____   vague   _____

league   _____   vogue   _____

Sound Activities - Extension Exercises

Crossword

-gue

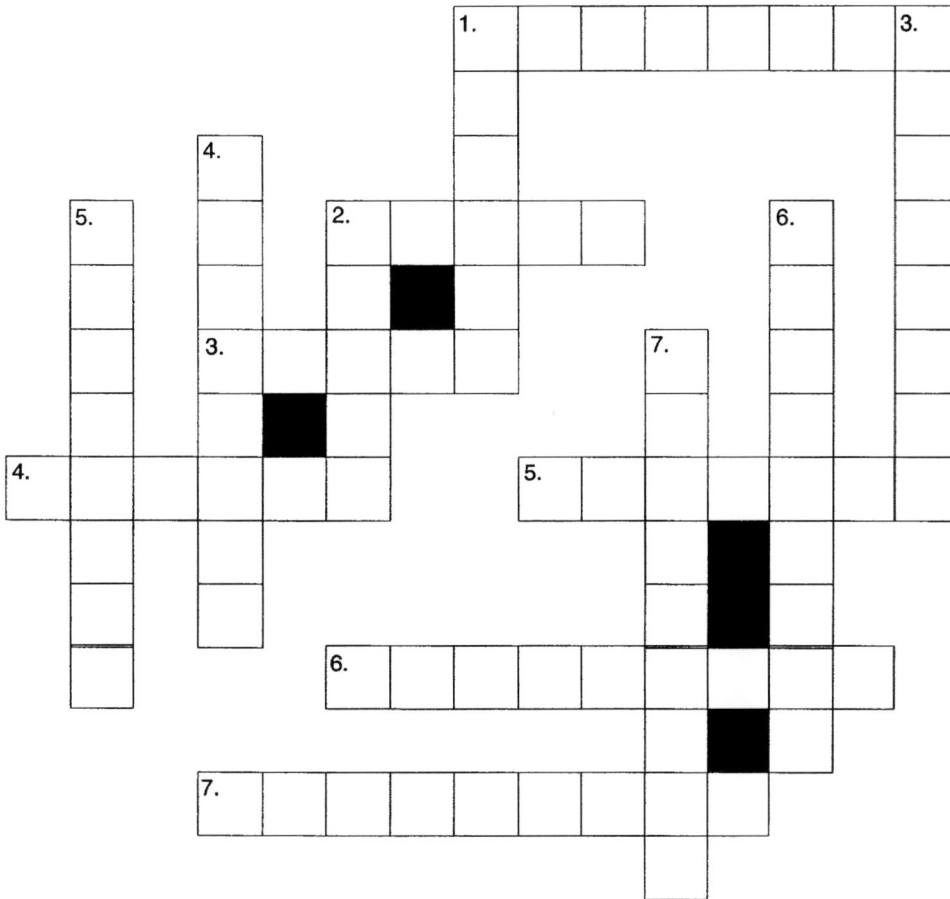

Across:

1. An introduction to a play.

2. Not clear; indistinct; uncertain.

3. A mischievous person; a scoundrel.

4. The organ used for tasting.

5. Tiredness.

6. A long speech made by one person; a scene in a play when only one person speaks.

7. A fellow worker.

Down:

1. A widespread disease which kills many people.

2. Fashion.

3. A speech to end a play; a short chapter to end a book.

4 To make a secret plan; to make someone curious.

5. A conversation.

6. A building for Jewish worship.

7. A descriptive list of items for sale.

vague	dialogue	fatigue	prologue	catalogue	plague	vogue
monologue	intrigue	tongue	synagogue	epilogue	colleague	rogue

34b

Mixed Bag

-gue

Synonyms

From the words below, find 12 pairs of words which have similar meanings. If you are not sure, use your dictionary or thesaurus to help you.

plague	dialogue	tiredness	indistinct	intrigue
vogue	cheat	vague	colleague	conversation
disease	fashion	rogue	workmate	fatigue
list	prologue	accent	plot	postscript
catalogue	brogue	introduction	epilogue	

1. _____ _____   7. _____ _____

2. _____ _____   8. _____ _____

3. _____ _____   9. _____ _____

4. _____ _____   10. _____ _____

5. _____ _____   11. _____ _____

6. _____ _____   12. _____ _____

Find the Mystery Word

The following words fit the squares below. Some letters have been given to help you. When you have completed the boxes, a mystery word will be revealed.

fatigue	plague	colleague	prologue	intrigue
	synagogue	vague	brogue	dialogue

You shouldn't be feeling listless if you've got the answer!_____

34c

Wordsearch

-ette

```
r o u l e t t e s t r e v m i
n a p a l e t t e h a t a i s
s h i w h e b a r a b i c p i
r e p a z t s f v c a q o e l
o m e l e t t e i e g u u t h
s l t g a e t t e t u e r t o
e a t c a s s e t t e t g e u
t y e g a z e t t e t e k e
t e m a r i o n e t t e t r t
e t a y e t t e n t e t t e t
m t l a u n d e r e t t e s e
p e t t e m a i s o n e t t e
```

Find each hidden word and write it on the line provided.
Use the LOOK, SAY, COVER, WRITE, CHECK method.

baguette   _____   marionette   _____

cassette   _____   omelette   _____

courgette   _____   palette   _____

etiquette   _____   pipette   _____

gazette   _____   rosette   _____

launderette   _____   roulette   _____

layette   _____   serviette   _____

maisonette   _____   silhouette   _____

Sound Activities - Extension Exercises

Name............................... Date.................................

Crossword

-ette

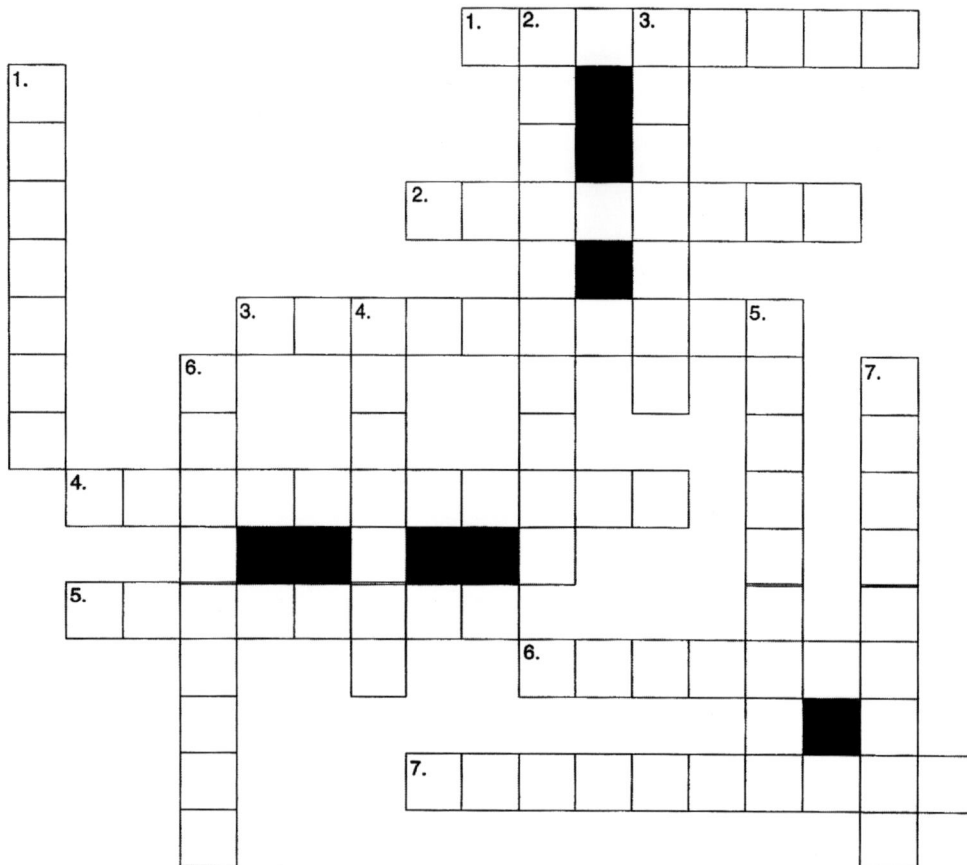

Across:

1. Beaten eggs, fried and folded.

2. A plastic case containing a recording tape.

3. A puppet on strings.

4. A shop with washing machines where people can do their washing.

5. A long, narrow loaf of bread.

6. A narrow tube used in science for measuring and moving liquid from one place to another.

7. The outline only of something, usually filled with black.

Down:

1. A board on which to mix paints.

2. A building in which to live, similar to a flat.

3. A set of clothing and articles for a new-born baby.

4. A badge made of ribbons, shaped like a rose.

5. Rules of how to behave socially.

6. Vegetable like a small marrow.

7. A table-napkin.

cassette   launderette   palette   pipette   etiquette   silhouette   marionette
maisonette   courgette   baguette   serviette   rosette   layette   omelette

35b

Mixed Bag   -ette

Word Within Words

Solve the clue and write the word from the following list which has the answer inside it. The first one has been done for you.

~~baguette~~	omelette	gazette	palette	launderette	maisonette
pipette	courgette	cassette	marionette	rosette	layette

1. a container made of soft material — b a g u e t t e

2. opposite of over — _ _ _ _ _ _ _ _ _ _ _

3. to look at; to stare — _ _ _ _ _ _ _

4. opposite of daughter — _ _ _ _ _ _ _ _ _ _

5. light in colour — _ _ _ _ _ _ _

6. a long, thin tube — _ _ _ _ _ _ _

7. a flower — _ _ _ _ _ _ _

8. a girl's name — _ _ _ _ _ _ _ _ _ _

9. belonging to us — _ _ _ _ _ _ _ _

10. up to the present time — _ _ _ _ _ _ _

11. a collection of things — _ _ _ _ _ _ _ _

12. to allow — _ _ _ _ _ _ _ _

Definitions

Use your dictionary to find out the meaning of each of these words.

gazette _____

_____

suffragette _____

_____

roulette _____

_____

leatherette _____

_____

usherette _____

_____

etiquette _____

_____

Name............................... Date.....................................

Wordsearch

```
d  p  r  g  c  o  n  n  o  i  s  s  e  u  r
i  a  s  r  h  u  o  s  z  e  u  r  n  a  v
s  c  h  a  u  f  f  e  u  r  x  d  t  g  a
t  r  e  n  p  e  d  c  o  n  e  u  r  r  m
a  c  f  d  k  u  w  a  t  r  i  s  e  a  a
h  o  s  e  u  r  a  t  f  f  e  l  p  v  t
a  i  t  u  m  t  h  e  u  r  u  e  r  u  e
s  f  e  r  l  i  q  u  e  u  r  o  e  l  u
e  f  u  k  g  e  u  r  l  e  c  i  n  e  r
u  e  r  i  m  a  s  s  e  u  r  s  e  u  n
r  u  b  n  e  c  h  e  u  r  f  e  u  r  o
t  r  u  f  i  s  a  b  o  t  e  u  r  m  k
```

Find each hidden word and write it on the line provided.
Use the LOOK, SAY, COVER, WRITE, CHECK method.

amateur _____   grandeur _____

chauffeur _____   liqueur _____

coiffeur _____   masseur _____

connoisseur _____   saboteur _____

entrepreneur _____   secateurs _____

36a

Name............................... Date.....................................

Crossword

-eur

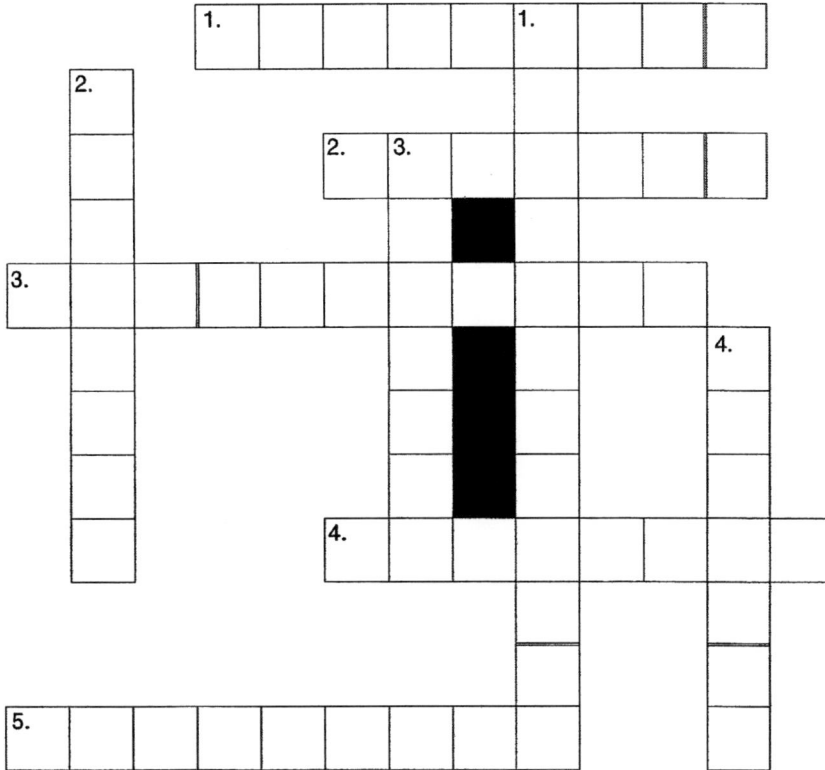

Across:

1. Clippers for pruning plants.

2. Someone who does something as a pastime, not as a job.

3. Someone who has enormous appreciation and experience of something.

4. Splendour; grandness.

5. Someone whose job is to drive another person's car.

Down:

1. Someone who sets up in business.

2. Someone who causes damage deliberately to hinder the enemy.

3. Someone who gives massages.

4. A very sweet type of alcoholic drink.

grandeur   chauffeur   saboteur   secateurs
entrepreneur   liqueur   connoisseur   masseur   amateur

36b

Mixed Bag
-eur

Definitions

Use your dictionary to find the meaning of each of these words.

coiffeur : _____

raconteur : _____

Syllables

Splitting a word into its syllables can often help you with its spelling. Split up the following words into syllables. You will have to decide if it has 2 or 3 syllables.

	1st	2nd	3rd
connoisseur			
chauffeur			
saboteur			
grandeur			
amateur			
secateurs			

A Cut Above the Rest

You have been given the word 'secateurs'. Can you fit the following words around it?

grandeur   saboteur   masseur   connoisseur   coiffeur   liqueur
entrepreneur   chauffeur   amateur

36c

Wordsearch

-cian

```
m  u  r  t  a  g  l  i  c  i  a  n  d  e  p  c
e  x  o  s  e  h  b  e  a  u  m  i  c  i  a  n
l  h  p  p  l  o  e  n  f  e  c  m  t  p  e  r
m  a  t  h  e  m  a  t  i  c  i  a  n  o  d  p
u  m  i  y  c  y  u  c  h  o  a  g  b  l  i  s
s  o  c  o  t  c  t  e  c  h  n  i  c  i  a  n
i  r  i  d  r  i  i  u  i  g  a  c  i  t  t  a
c  t  a  r  i  a  c  t  a  y  k  i  a  i  r  d
i  i  n  i  c  n  i  l  n  s  h  a  n  c  i  c
a  c  x  c  i  l  a  m  c  i  a  n  o  i  c  i
n  i  e  i  a  n  n  t  e  f  m  a  h  a  i  a
s  a  p  a  n  p  h  y  s  i  c  i  a  n  a  n
h  n  r  s  t  a  t  i  s  t  i  c  i  a  n  d
```

Find each hidden word and write it on the line provided.
Use the LOOK, SAY, COVER, WRITE, CHECK method.

beautician	_____	optician	_____
electrician	_____	paediatrician	_____
magician	_____	physician	_____
mathematician	_____	politician	_____
mortician	_____	statistician	_____
musician	_____	technician	_____

37a

Name............................. Date...................................

Crossword

-cian

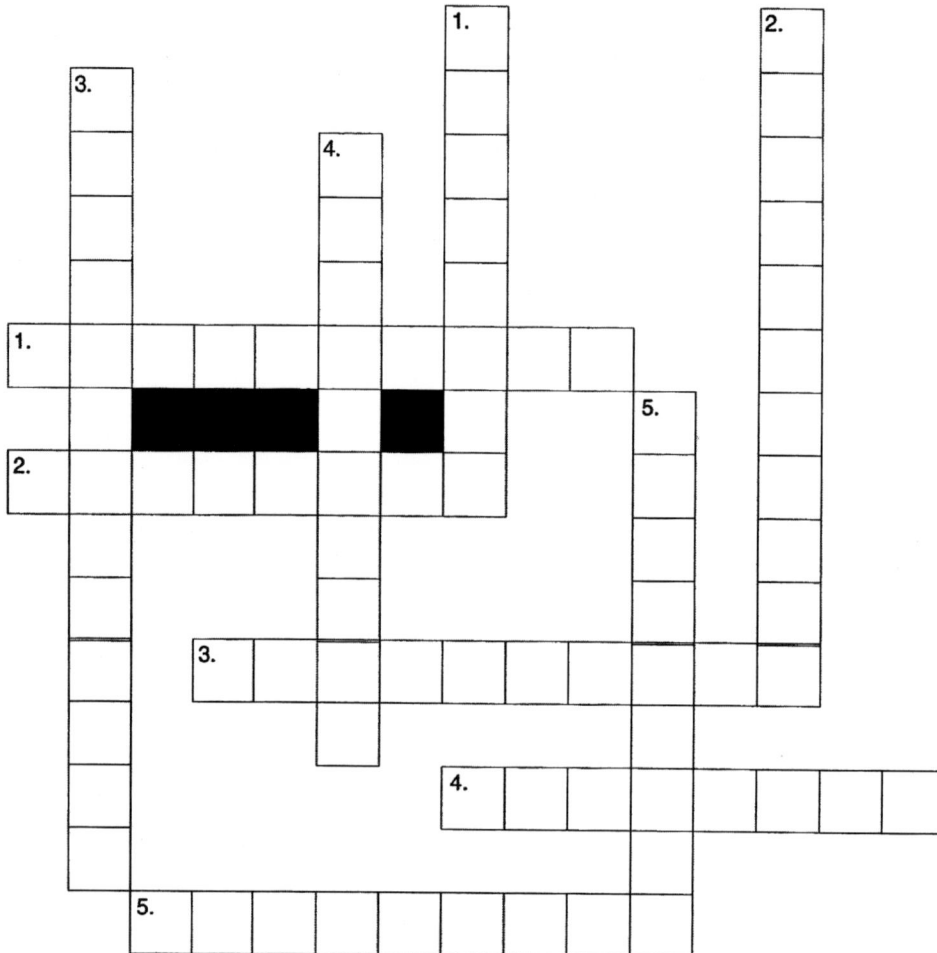

Across:

1. A person whose job is to look after equipment in a laboratory.

2. A wizard.

3. Someone who gives beautifying treatments to the body and face.

4. Someone who plays a musical instrument.

5. American word for undertaker.

Down:

1. A person who makes spectacles.

2. A person who repairs and installs electrical equipment.

3. A person skilled in making maths calculations.

4. Someone whose job is in politics.

5. A doctor.

electrician   mathematician   optician   technician   musician
politician   beautician   magician   physician   mortician

37b

Mixed Bag

-cian

What's My Line?

The suffix '-cian' (pronounced 'shan') is used for someone who is an expert in something. Can you solve these riddles to find out what each person does?

1. I try never to lose my key;
    Some days I might feel plucky;
    On others I might blow my own trumpet;
    I always make notes of what I'm doing
    In order to strike the right chord.

    I'm a _____

2. I never lose sight of what I'm doing,
    Even if I'm not in the right frame.
    I always make spectacles of myself;
    If you don't see me, you might need your eyes tested.

    I'm an _____

3. I like to make light work of things
    And try not to get my wires crossed.
    My job is one of power,
    But what I do shouldn't shock you.

    I'm an _____

The Experts

Pair up the expert with what he or she is an expert in.
The first one has been done for you.

music   mathematician   magic   electrician   paediatrics
mathematics   musician politician   electrics   magician   paediatrician   politics

_____music_____   _____musician_____

_____   _____

_____   _____

_____   _____

_____   _____

_____   _____

Sound Activities - Extension Exercises

Wordsearch Answers

1a ar (air)

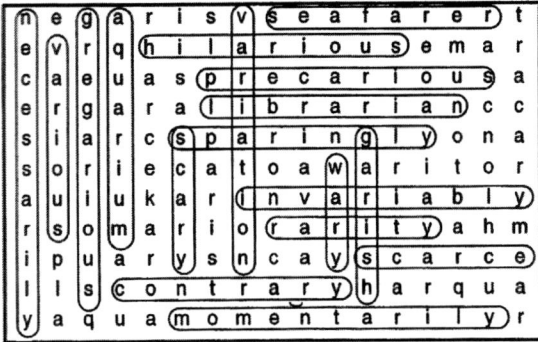

2a ear (er)

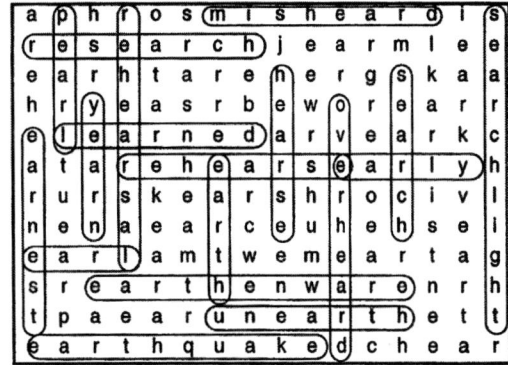

3a o (ŭ)

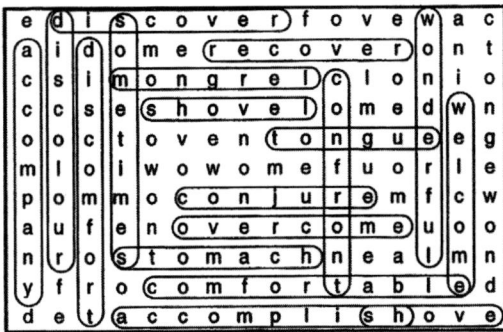

4a Silent t

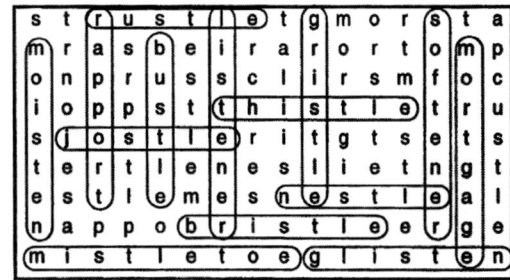

5a ee

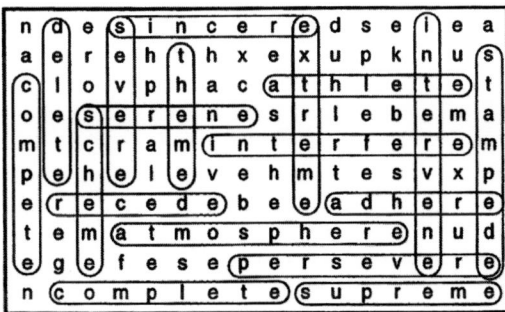

6a igh

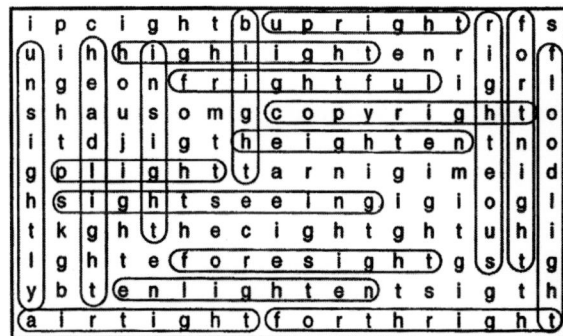

7a are (air)

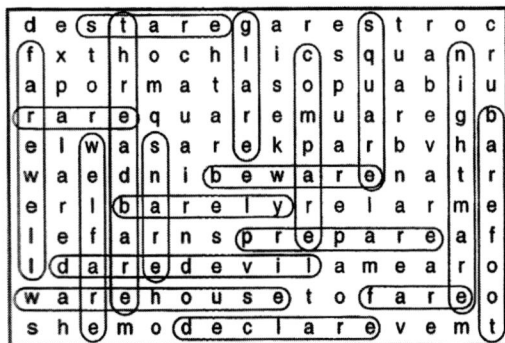

8a cc (hard c / soft c)

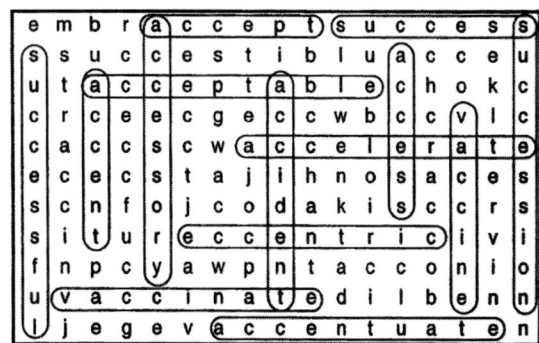

Wordsearch Answers

9a ph

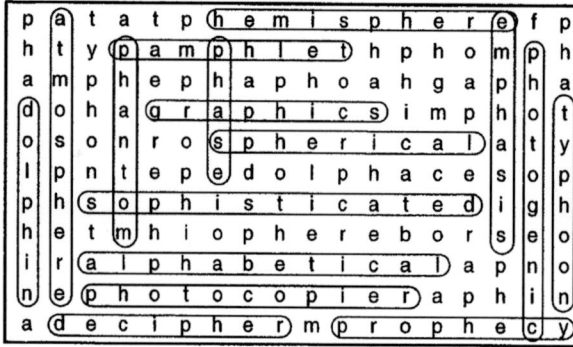

10a cc (hard c)

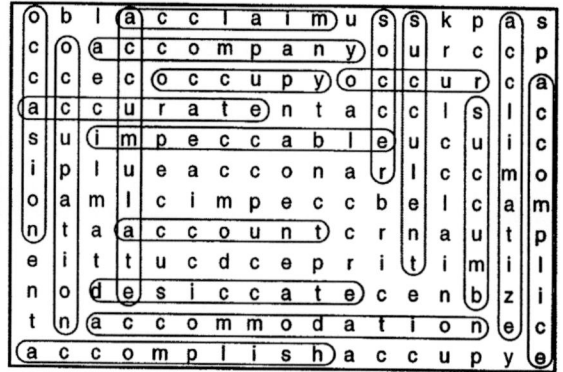

11a ui (oo)

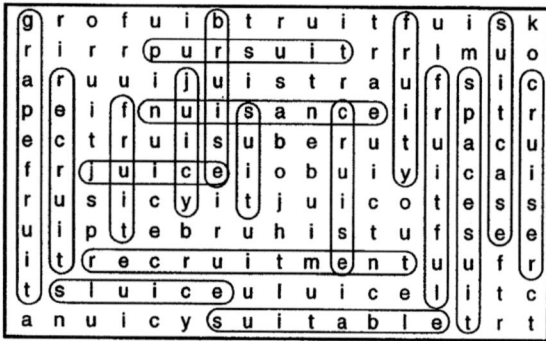

12a ey (ā)

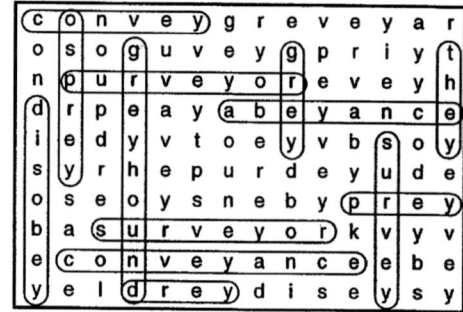

13a Silent g

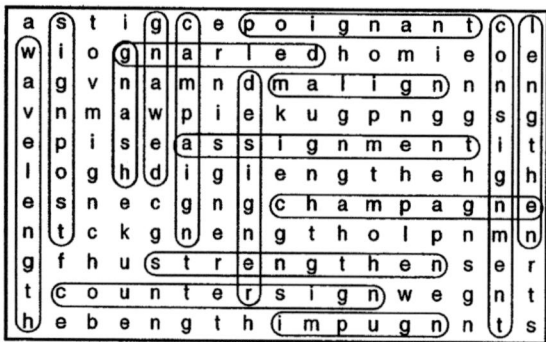

14a ou (oo)

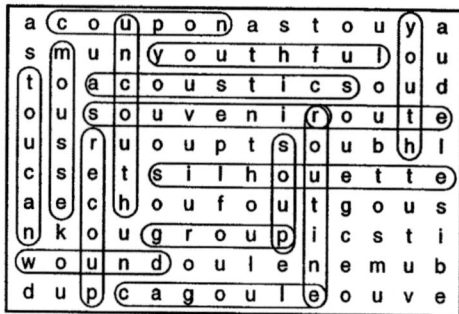

15a a (ŏ)

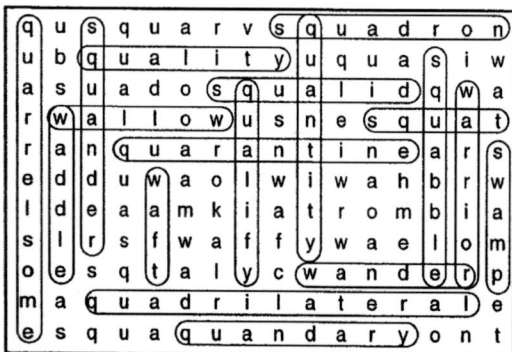

16a sc (s followed by soft c)

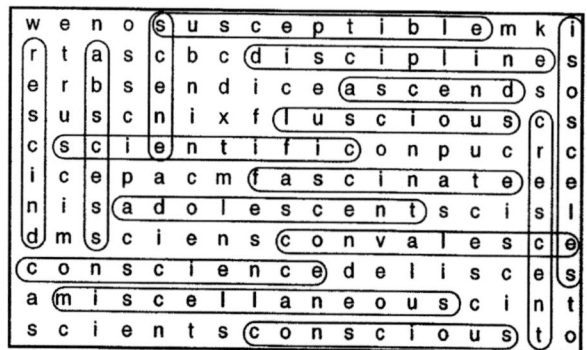

Wordsearch Answers

17a ch (sh)

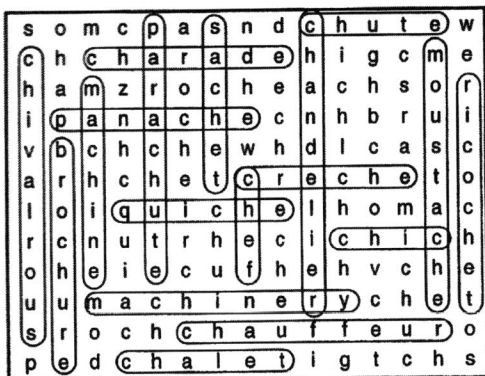

18a eu (u)

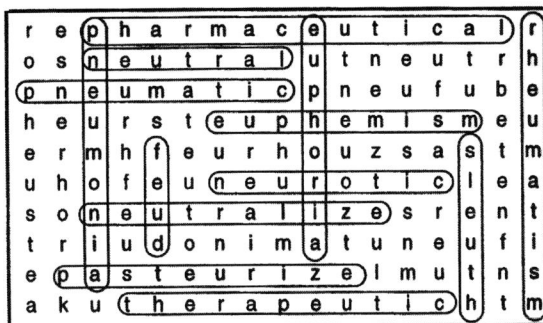

19a Silent letters b, h, s, w

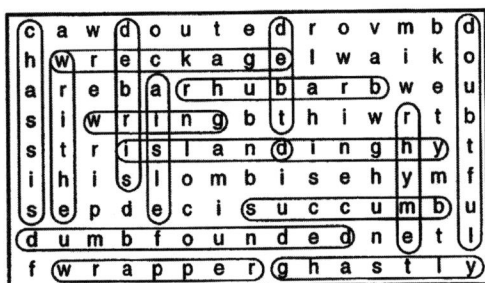

20a - ee

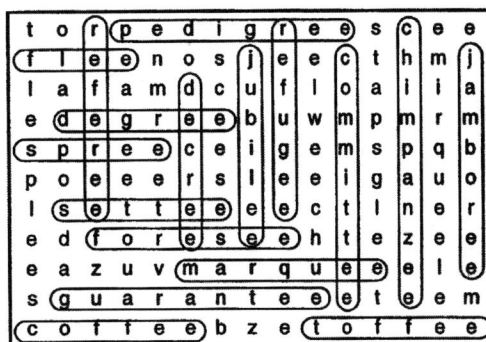

21a -eous

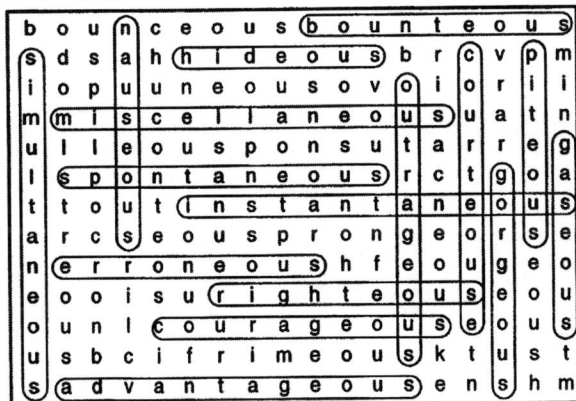

22a -re

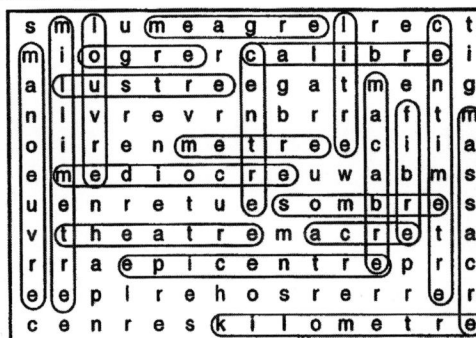

23a -que

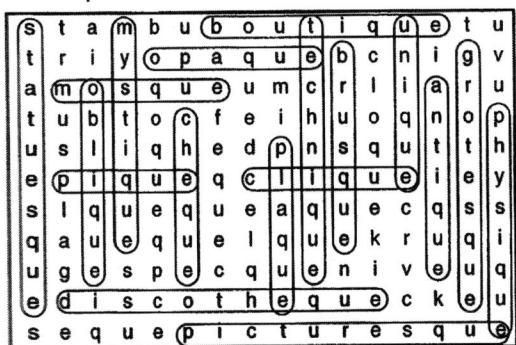

24a -el

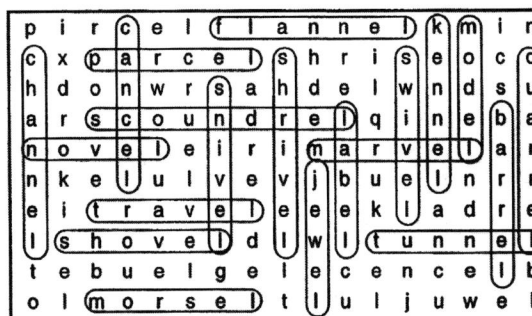

Wordsearch Answers

25a -et (ay)

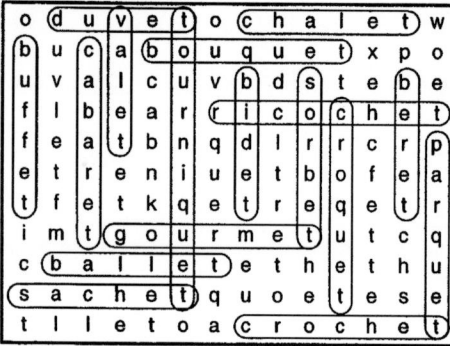

26a -ey (ē)

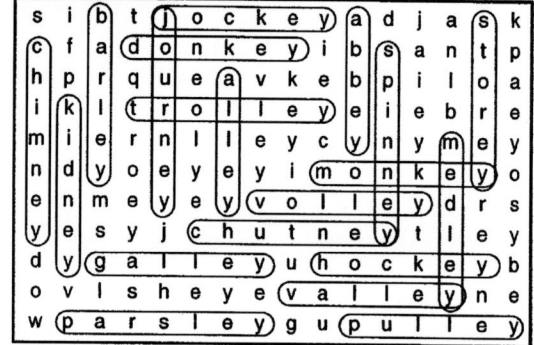

27a -a

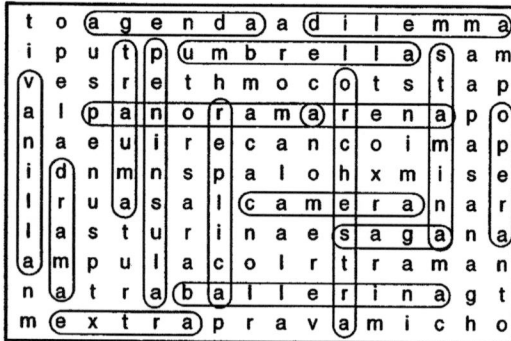

28a -i (ē)

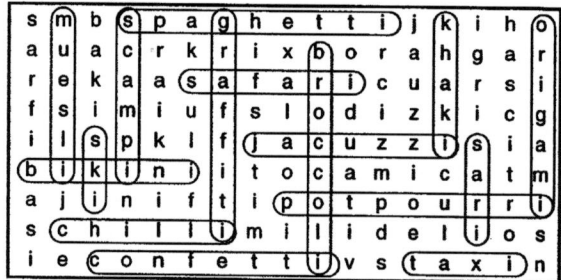

29a -o (ō)

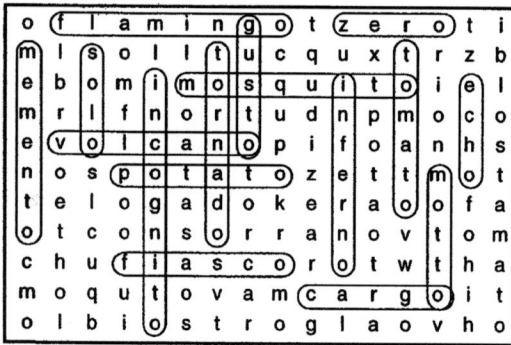

30a -ē, -ī and -ū

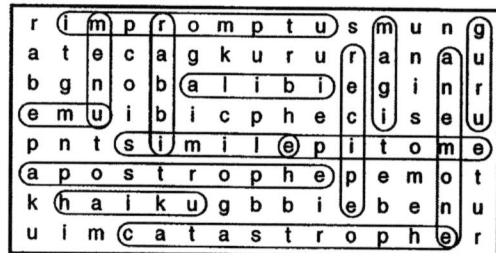

31a -tial

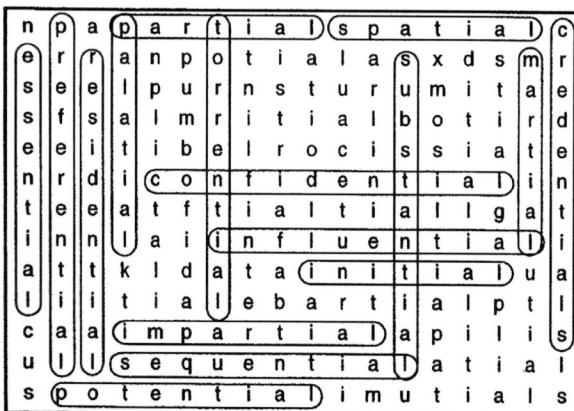

Wordsearch Answers

32a -cial

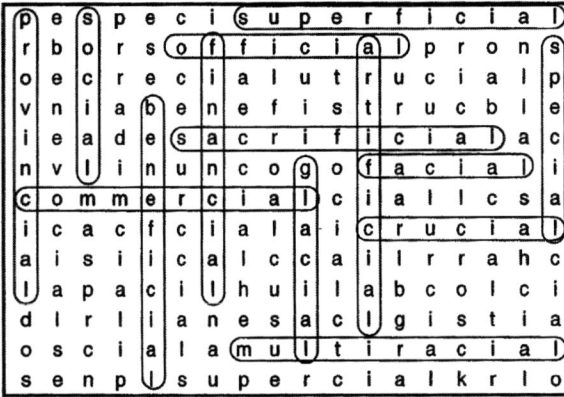

33a -eon

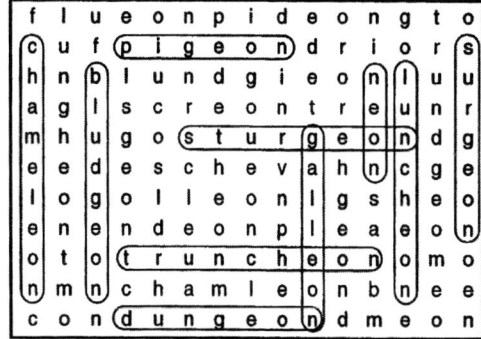

34a -gue

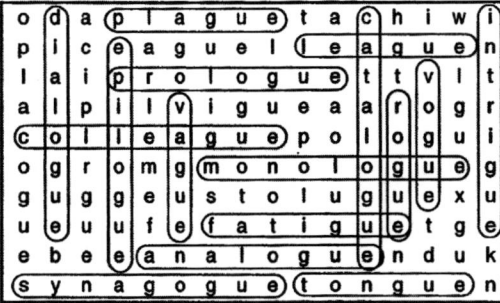

35a -ette

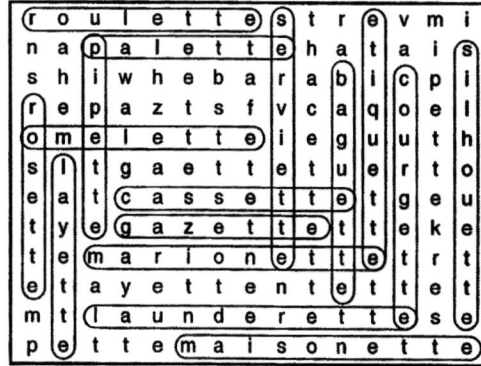

36a -eur

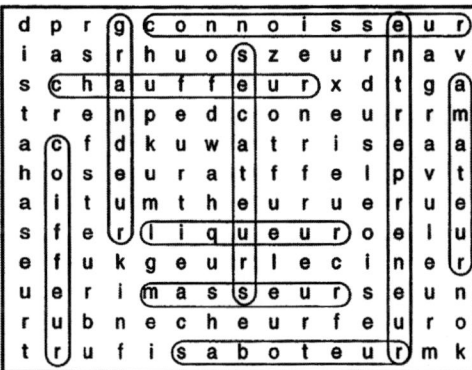

37a -cian

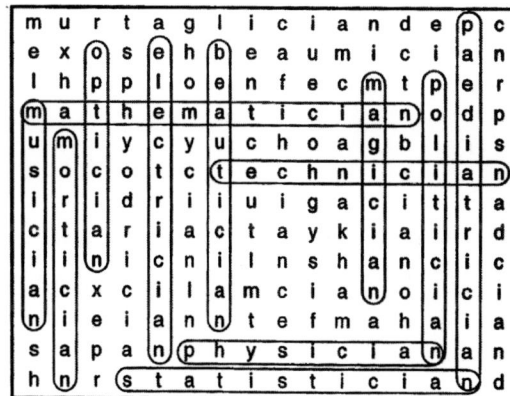

Crossword Answers

1.b ar (air)

Across: 1. various; 2. garish; 3. scarce; 4. aquarium; 5. contrary; 6. sparingly;
7. invariably
Down: 1. rarity; 2. gregarious; 3. hilarious; 4. precarious; 5. librarian; 6. wary; 7. scary

2.b ear (er)

Across: 1. early; 2. overheard; 3. rehearse; 4. search; 5. yearn; 6. pearl;
7. earthenware
Down: 1. earnest; 2. unearth; 3. research; 4, learned; 5. hearse; 6. earthquake; 7. Earth

3.b o (u)

Across: 1. discolour; 2. recover; 3. mongrel; 4. conjure; 5. shovel; 6. stomach
Down: 1. accomplish; 2. welcome; 3. tongue; 4. confront; 5. wonderful; 6. accompany

4.b Silent t

Across: 1. debut; 2. depot; 3. bustle; 4. glisten; 5. jostle; 6. gristle; 7. listener
Down: 1. rapport; 2. mortgage; 3. bristle; 4. rustle; 5. thistle; 6. nestle; 7. mistletoe

5.b e e

Across: 1. atmosphere; 2. recede; 3. sincere; 4. serene; 5. athlete; 6. supreme;
7. extreme
Down: 1. adhere; 2. persevere; 3. stampede; 4. severe; 5. complete; 6. compete;
7. intervene

6.b igh

Across: 1. unsightly; 2. sightseeing; 3. floodlight; 4. blight; 5. fortnight; 6. airtight
Down: 1. upright; 2. heighten; 3. insight; 4. highlight; 5. forthright; 6. plight

7.b are (air)

Across: 1. warehouse; 2. barefoot; 3. stare; 4. prepare; 5. welfare; 6. glare; 7. barely
Down: 1. beware; 2. threadbare; 3. snare; 4. nightmare; 5. declare; 6. compare;
7. farewell

8.b cc (hard c / soft c)

Across: 1. accessory; 2. vaccine; 3. accelerate; 4. successful; 5. accident; 6. eccentric
Down: 1. succession; 2. vaccinate; 3. accent; 4. accentuate; 5. access; 6. accept

9.b ph

Across: 1. sophisticated; 2. photogenic; 3. atmosphere; 4. dolphin; 5. graphics;
6. pamphlet; 7. phase
Down: 1. spherical; 2. decipher; 3. typhoon; 4. photocopier; 5. emphasis; 6. prophecy

10.b. cc (hard c)

Across: 1. accomplice; 2. accompany; 3. occur; 4. accurate; 5. account; 6. accomplish
Down: 1. occasion; 2. impeccable; 3. occupation; 4. succulent; 5. accumulate;
6. succumb

11.b ui (oo)

Across: 1. pursuit; 2. fruit; 3. bruise; 4. suitable; 5. juice; 6. suitcase; 7. juicy
Down: 1. grapefruit; 2. fruitful; 3. sluice; 4. spacesuit; 5. recruit; 6. cruise; 7. nuisance

Crossword Answers

12.b ey (ā)
Across: 1. grey; 2. survey; 3. convey; 4. osprey; 5. drey; 6. disobey
Down: 1. greyhound; 2. abeyance; 3. purveyor; 4. they; 5. surveyor; 6. prey

13.b Silent g
Across: 1. impugn; 2. countersign; 3. gnaw; 4. designer; 5. poignant; 6. signpost
Down: 1. lengthen; 2. consignment; 3. gnarled; 4. assignment; 5. malign; 6. gnash

14.b ou (oo)
Across: 1. route; 2. recoup; 3. uncouth; 4. mousse; 5. silhouette; 6. cagoule;
7. souvenir
Down: 1. youth; 2. routine; 3. coupon; 4. group; 5. youthful; 6. acoustics; 7. toucan

15.b a (ŏ)
Across: 1. squander; 2. squat; 3. squalid; 4. waft; 5. quarantine; 6. waddle; 7. quality
Down: 1. quantity; 2. quadrilateral; 3. squabble; 4. wallow; 5. qualify; 6. quandary;
7. wander

16.b sc (s followed by soft c)
Across: 1. rescind; 2. scene; 3. fascinate; 4. adolescent; 5. susceptible; 6. convalesce
Down: 1. scientific; 2. conscious; 3. crescent; 4. ascend; 5. luscious; 6. discipline

17.b ch (sh)
Across: 1. parachute; 2. machinery; 3. charades; 4. sachet; 5. chauffeur; 6. creche;
7. panache
Down: 1. quiche; 2. moustache; 3. chute; 4. machine; 5. brochure; 6. chic; 7. ricochet

18.b eu (ū)
Across: 1. pharmaceutical; 2. therapeutic; 3. pneumonia; 4. rheumatism; 5. feud;
6. neurotic
Down: 1. pasteurize; 2. euphoria; 3. Europe; 4. neutral; 5. pneumatic; 6. sleuth

19.b Silent letters (b, h, s, w)
Across: 1. dinghy; 2. writhe; 3. dumbfounded; 4. wrapper; 5. island; 6. ghastly;
7. rhubarb
Down: 1. doubtful; 2. wreckage; 3. debt; 4. wring; 5. succumb; 6. chassis; 7. aisle;
8. debris

20.b -ee
Across: 1. degree; 2. glee; 3. refugee; 4. flee; 5. settee; 6. marquee; 7. pedigree
Down: 1. decree; 2. guarantee; 3. jamboree; 4. committee; 5. spree; 6. jubilee;
7. referee

21.b -eous
Across: 1. erroneous; 2. courteous; 3. spontaneous; 4. miscellaneous; 5. courageous;
6. nauseous
Down: 1. piteous; 2. gorgeous; 3. bounteous; 4. instantaneous; 5. hideous;
6. simultaneous

22.b -re
Across: 1. macabre; 2. lustre; 3. massacre; 4. centimetre; 5. litre; 6. ogre; 7. mediocre
Down: 1. meagre; 2. sombre; 3. acre; 4. centre; 5. fibre; 6. theatre; 7. mitre

Crossword Answers

23.b -que
Across: 1. boutique; 2. picturesque; 3. opaque; 4. pique; 5. technique; 6. brusque
Down: 1. grotesque; 2. mystique; 3. oblique; 4. plaque; 5. cheque; 6. antique; 7. unique

24.b -el
Across: 1. marvel; 2. cancel; 3. channel; 4. shrivel; 5. label; 6. scoundrel; 7. swivel
Down: 1. morsel; 2. barrel; 3. jewel; 4. flannel; 5. shovel; 6. parcel; 7. novel

25.b -et (ay)
Across: 1. sachet; 2.ballet; 3. gourmet; 4. tourniquet; 5. buffet; 6. cabaret; 7. sorbet
Down: 1. chalet; 2. beret; 3. bouquet; 4. parquet; 5. ricochet; 6. duvet; 7. croquet

26.b -ey (ē)
Across: 1. storey; 2. journey; 3. chimney; 4. pulley; 5. chutney; 6. galley; 7. alley;
8. parsley
Down: 1. trolley; 2. hockey; 3. kidney; 4. spinney; 5. jockey; 6. valley

27.b -a
Across: 1. replica; 2. agenda; 3. vanilla; 4. saga; 5. umbrella; 6. trauma; 7. stamina
Down: 1. peninsula; 2. arena; 3. panorama; 4. extra; 5. dilemma; 6. aroma; 7. drama

28.b -i (ē)
Across: 1. scampi; 2. confetti; 3. origami; 4. muesli; 5. graffiti; 6. broccoli; 7. khaki
Down: 1. spaghetti; 2. jacuzzi; 3. pot-pourri; 4. taxi; 5. safari; 6. bikini; 7. sari

29.b -o (ō)
Across: 1. mosquito 2. memento; 3. volcano; 4. incognito; 5. fiasco; 6.gusto; 7. solo
Down: 1. zero; 2. tornado; 3. motto; 4. inferno; 5. flamingo; 6. cargo; 7. echo

30.b -ē, -ī and -ū
Across: 1. simile; 2. haiku; 3. guru; 4. catastrophe; 5. epitome; 6. impromptu;
7. anemone
Down: 1. menu; 2. Magi; 3. apostrophe; 4. recipe; 5. alibi ; 6. rabbi; 7. emu

31.b -tial
Across: 1. palatial; 2. essential; 3. partial;4. substantial; 5. confidential; 6. sequential
Down: 1. potential; 2. initial; 3. credentials; 4. torrential; 5. influential; 6. martial

32.b -cial
Across: 1. commercial; 2. social; 3. sacrificial; 4. artificial; 5. crucial
Down: 1. beneficial; 2. special; 3. financial; 4. official; 5. multiracial; 6. facial

33.b -eon
Across: 1. pigeon; 2. sturgeon; 3. chameleon; 4. surgeon; 5. luncheon
Down: 1. dungeon; 2. truncheon; 3. bludgeon; 4. galleon; 5. neon

34.b -gue
Across: 1. prologue; 2. vague; 3. rogue; 4. tongue; 5. fatigue; 6. monologue;
7. colleague
Down: 1. plague; 2. vogue; 3. epilogue; 4. intrigue; 5. dialogue; 6. synagogue;
7. catalogue

Crossword Answers

35.b -ette

Across: 1. omelette; 2. cassette; 3. marionette; 4. launderette; 5. baguette; 6. pipette; 7. silhouette

Down: 1. palette; 2. maisonette; 3. layette; 4. rosette; 5. etiquette; 6. courgette; 7. serviette

36.b -eur

Across: 1. secateurs; 2. amateur; 3. connoisseur; 4. grandeur; 5. chauffeur

Down: 1. entrepreneur; 2. saboteur; 3. masseur; 4. liqueur

37.b -cian

Across: 1. technician; 2. magician; 3. beautician; 4. musician; 5. mortician

Down: 1. optician; 2. electrician; 3. mathematician; 4. politician; 5. physician

Mixed Bag Answers

1c. ar (air)

Antonyms

scarce/ plentiful; safe/ precarious; abundance/ scarcity; variable/ constant;
gregarious/ solitary; wary/ trusting; lavish/ sparing; quiet/ garish

Some General Knowledge Questions

1. mosquito; 2. Tutankhamun; 3. King Henry VIII; 4. ram (male sheep)
5. 100 years or over; 6. meat; 7. a room in which to enjoy the rays of the sun; 8. Africa;
9. Europe; 10. Budapest; 11. Captain James Cook; 12. of water

Odd One Out : aquarium - not a zodiac sign

2c. ear (er)

Words Within Words

1. re<u>hear</u>se; 2. <u>ear</u>th; 3. un<u>ear</u>th; 4. <u>yearn</u>; 5. ear<u>then</u>ware; 6. ear<u>nest</u>; 7. rese<u>arch</u>;
8. h<u>ears</u>e; 9. <u>pearl</u>; 10. <u>early</u>; 11. mi<u>sheard</u>; 12. se<u>arch</u>

Synonyms:

earthenware/ pottery; research/ investigate; educated/ learned; hunt/ search;
rehearse/ practise; earth/ soil; long/ yearn; unearth/ discover; sincere/ earnest;
premature/ early

Find the Words: earth; art; ware; are; then; the; hen; war; ear; he

A Proverb : Someone who acts promptly is more likely to be successful in getting what
he or she wants.

3c. o (ŭ)

Some General Knowledge Questions

1. monastery; 2. witches; 3. red; 4. 13; 5. digests food; 6. Devon, Dorset, Wiltshire, Avon;
7. turn head over heels in the air and land on feet; 8. day of the moon

Idioms

to have money to burn/ to have so much money that it doesn't matter if it's wasted;
money for old rope / money earned for little or no effort; to spend money like water/ to
spend a lot of money unnecessarily; money talks/ people with a lot of money have power
and influence to get what they want; to throw good money after bad/ to spend a lot of
money in an attempt to regain money already lost

Words Within Words : comfort; fort; for; or; table; tab; able

4c. Silent t

Anagrams

1. RAPPORT; 2. MORTGAGE; 3. THISTLE; 4. BRISTLE; 5. RUSTLE; 6. BUSTLE;
7. JOSTLE 8. MISTLETOE; 9. SOFTENER; 10. GRISTLE

Idioms:

1. to have a drink; 2. to make something quickly; 3. to have unrealistic plans for the future

Words Within Words: 1. bu<u>st</u>le; 2. de<u>po</u>t; 3. mi<u>st</u>letoe; 4. <u>rust</u>le; 5. de<u>but</u>; 6. rap<u>port</u>

5c. e‿e

Solve me - if you can! : adhere

Nouns and Adjectives

atmosphere/ atmospheric; serenity/ serene; athlete/ athletic; supremacy/ supreme;
extremity/ extreme; sincerity/ sincere; severity/ severe

Countries and People

China/ Chinese; Japan/ Japanese; Vietnam/ Vietnamese; Portugal/ Portuguese;
Lebanon/ Lebanese; Sudan/ Sudanese; Burma/ Burmese; Malta/ Maltese

Mixed Bag Answers

6c. igh

Homophones

1. side/ sighed; 2. write/ right/ rite; 3. night/ knight; 4. incite/ insight; 5. Titan/ tighten;
6. might/ mite; 7. higher/ hire; 8. size/ sighs; 9. sight/ site/ cite; 10. sleight/ slight

lightning : a flash of electricity produced during a thunderstorm

lightening : making less heavy; becoming less dark

Similes : 1. lightning; 2. light; 3. right; 4. tight

Idioms

to keep a tight rein on something/ to keep something under control;

in a tight corner/ to be in a difficult situation;

to tighten ones belt/ to spend less money and be careful with it;

for the high jump/ about to be severely punished;

as right as rain / feeling fit and healthy; right up your street/ the kind of thing you like to know about;

in the limelight / to be the centre of public attention; highway robbery / to pay far too much for something

7c. are (air)

Homophones

mare : a female horse

mayor : person in charge of a town council

flare : a sudden, bright flame; to burn with a sudden bright flame

flair: an instinct for something

fare : a charge made for travelling on transport

fair: just; light-coloured; outdoor entertainments; quite good

compare : to liken something to something else

compere : someone who introduces performers in a show

pare : to cut away or trim the surface of something

pair : two of something

pear : a fruit

hair : fine filaments which grow from many animals' skin

hare: a mammal similar to a rabbit

Idioms :

1. a balanced and nutritious meal; 2. a fair and honest deal or bargain;
3. to start again at the beginning

A Cryptic Clue : nightmare

8c. cc (hard c / soft c)

Verbs and Nouns : accelerate/acceleration; accept/acceptance; succeed/success; accentuate/accentuation; accede/accession; vaccinate/vaccination

Confusing Words :

accept : to take something which is offered

except: omitting; leaving out

access : the way in; to be able to use data on a computer

excess : an extra amount

accent : the manner in which a word is pronounced

ascent : an upward climb

accede : to enter into office; to come to the throne

exceed : to go beyond

The Right Word : 1. accept; 2. access; 3. accent; 4. accede

Mixed Bag Answers

9c. ph

Phone Home! :
1. telephone; 2. saxophone; 3. headphones; 4. megaphone; 5. xylophone

The Suffix '-graph'
1. paragraph; 2. photograph; 3. seismograph; 4. autograph; 5. telegraph
————— written or drawn

'Graphy' words :
1. geography; 2. calligraphy; 3. biography; 4. photography; 5. autobiography

10c. cc (hard c)

Synonyms
occasion/ event; accompany/ escort; exact/ accurate; lodgings/ accommodation; accomplice/ partner; succulent/ juicy; happen/ occur; occupation/ job; football/ soccer; report/ account; familiar/ accustomed; accomplish/ achieve; blame/ accuse; collect/ accumulate

Definitions
desiccate : remove moisture from
acclaim : to welcome or applaud enthusiastically
acclimatize : to become used to new surroundings or climate
account : a bill; a statement of money received and spent; a story or description; to explain

How Many Words Can You 'Accumulate'?
assemble; gather; accrue; collect; amass; muster

11c. ui (oo)

Tailored to fit
1. suitcase; 2. spacesuit; 3. suitable; 4. swimsuit; 5. unsuitable; 6. suitability; 7. pursuit

Words Within Words
1. pur_suit_; 2. sui_table_; 3. recruit_ment_; 4. _space_suit; 5. slu_ice_; 6; cru_ise_; 7. gra_pe_fruit; 8. ju_icy_

Alphabetical Order: sluice; spacesuit; suitability; suitable; suitcase; suitor; swimsuit

12c. ey (ā)

Solve the Riddle: obey
Nouns: 1. conveyance; 2. obedience; 3. survey; 4. greyness; 5. disobedience
Some General Knowledge Questions
1. predator; 2. Dorset; 3. Iceland; 4. Indian; 5. a time when something is at its best
Change a Letter : grey; drey; prey

13c. Silent g

Find The Mystery Word:
1. designer; 2. campaign; 3. lengthen; 4. gnarl; 5. poignant; 6. countersign; 7. consign; 8. strength   Mystery word : signpost

Syllables:
count / er/ sign; de / sign/ er; streng / then; con / sign / ment; wave / length; re / sign
Sign Up Here! : 1. assign; 2. consign; 3. design; 4. ensign; 5. resign

Mixed Bag Answers

14c. ou (oo)

What Am I? : souvenir

Alphabetical Order : cartouche; coupon; goulash; group; routine; uncouth; you; youth

Anagrams:

1. ROUTINE; 2. UNCOUTH; 3. SILHOUETTE; 4. SOUVENIR; 5. TOUCAN; 6. SOUP; 7. ACOUSTICS; 8. ROUTE

Idioms :

1. in trouble or difficulties; 2. make a painful experience even more painful for someone

15c. a (ŏ)

Words beginning with 'quad-'

1. quadruped; 2. quadrilateral; 3. quadrant; 4. quadruplet; 5. quadruple - four

Odd One Out : waffle - is not a living creature

Words Within Words:

1. waddle; 2. wanted; 3. squalid; 4. quadrilateral; 5. wasp; 6. squash; 7. whatever; 8. swamp; 9. swallow; 10. what; 11. wallet; 12. wander

16c. sc (s followed by soft c)

Consonants and Vowels :

1. conscience; 2. luscious; 3. adolescent; 4. isosceles; 5. fascinate; 6. discipline

What goes up, must come down! :

1. descendant; 2. rescind; 3. scissors; 4. crescent; 5. scenery; 6. convalesce; 7. discern

Definitions : 1. discern - to understand clearly; to make out

2. descendant - a person who is descended from someone

Some General Knowledge Questions

1. a triangle with two equal sides; 2. an oriental curved sword; 3. The Scilly Isles

17c. ch (sh)

Some General Knowledge Questions

1. Illinois; 2. sit on it; 3. prepares and cooks food in a restaurant or hotel; 4. antelope; 5. on the ceiling; 6. a nut; 7. a composer; 8. Charles; 9. No, a person who pretends to have certain knowledge or skill

How Revealing! :

1. pistachio; 2. Charlotte; 3. brochure; 4. sachet; 5. chic; 6. chalet; 7. quiche; 8. moustache; 9. chef   Mystery word : parachute

18c. eu (ū)

Nouns and Adjectives

pharmacy/ pharmaceutical; therapy/ therapeutic; Europe/ European; euphoria/ euphoric; neurosis/ neurotic; rheumatism/ rheumatic

Some General Knowledge Questions

1. Sir Arthur Conan Doyle; 2. play a tune on it; 3. Louis Pasteur; 4. a tree; 5. Asia

Definitions :

1. euphemism - substitution of a mild expression for a more direct and blunt one;

2. eulogy - a speech or piece of writing in praise of someone;

3. neurology - scientific study of the nervous system

Mixed Bag Answers

19c. Silent letters (b, h, s, w)

The Silent Majority :

ghost; wriggle; honour; island; debris; doubt; comb; succumb; wrapper; wring; chassis; rhythm

Confusing Words: dinghy - a small boat; dingy - shabby and dirty looking; dinghy has a hard g sound because the g is followed by the letter h - dingy has a soft g sound because the g is followed by the letter y.

Anagrams:

1. RHYME; 2. ISLANDS; 3. WRITHES; 4. AISLES; 5. WRAPPING; 6. DEBRIS; 7. WRECKAGE; 8. RHINOCEROS; 9. SHIPWRECKED; 10. WRESTLE

20c. -ee

The Suffix '-ee' : 1. referee; 2. trustee; 3. absentee; 4. employee; 5. trainee; 6. nominee

Idioms

to see red / to become very angry; can't do something for toffee / to be very bad at doing something; something doesn't grow on trees / something is very scarce; to bark up the wrong tree / to follow a wrong course of action; to go down on bended knee / to beg for something; to be footloose and fancy-free / to have no responsibilities; to see which way the cat jumps / to wait to see how a situation develops; to get off scot-free / to escape punishment; to give someone a free rein / to allow someone freedom of action

21c. -eous

Nouns and Adjectives

outrage/ outrageous; instant / instantaneous; gas/ gaseous; courage/ courageous; pity/ piteous; error/ erroneous; miscellany/ miscellaneous; righteousness/ righteous; nausea/ nauseous; spontaneity/ spontaneous; advantage/ advantageous

Words Within Words:

1. spontaneous; 2. outrageous; 3. hideous; 4. righteous; 5. courteous; 6. nauseous; 7. miscellaneous; 8. piteous; 9. gorgeous; 10. advantageous

22c. -re

Some General Knowledge Questions

1. 100; 2. a bishop; 3. Paris; 4. a sword; 5. land; 6. radius; 7. 10; 8. 10

Nouns and Adjectives

fibre/ fibrous; centre/ central; theatre/ theatrical; mediocrity/ mediocre; lustre/ lustrous; ogre/ ogrish

Homophones : metre - the main unit of length in the metric system; meter - a measuring instrument

23c. -que

Synonyms and Antonyms:

1. opaque/ clouded/ transparent; 2. grotesque / repulsive/ charming; 3. unique / unequalled/ common; 4. brusque / abrupt/ polite; 5. antique/ old/ modern; 6. oblique/ slanting/ straight

What's in a Word?

1. discotheque; 2. ballet; 3. Muslims; 4. dignified like a statue; 5. sail in it

Homophones

cheque - a written order to a banker to pay money to someone; check - to make sure; a pattern of squares; to stop or control

Mixed Bag Answers

24c. -el

Change a Letter :

1. fennel; 2. vowel; 3. funnel; 4. duel; 5. gravel; 6. swivel; 7. cruel; 8. revel

Prefixes: 1. propel; 2. compel; 3. dispel; 4. repel; 5. impel; 6. expel

Homophones

1. kernel - the part inside the shell of a nut;
   colonel - a senior army officer who usually commands a regiment
2. duel - a fight or contest between two people;
   dual - having two parts; forming a pair
3. navel - small hollow in the centre of someone's abdomen where the umbilical cord was attached;
   naval - to do with the navy
4. mantel - a shelf over a fireplace;
   mantle - a cloak; a covering
5. counsel - advice or to give advice;
   council - a group of people elected to make decisions
6. mussel - a kind of shellfish;
   muscle - fibres which can contract to cause movement of the body

25c. -et (ay)

Missing Words: ballet; bouquet; gourmet; buffet; sorbet; parquet; chalet - French

Words Within Words

1. ballet; 2. chalet; 3. duvet; 4. cabaret; 5. buffet; 6. gourmet; 7. sorbet

26c. -ey (ē)

Odd One Out

1. carrot - not a cereal crop; 2. beach - not part of a ship; 3. cabbage - not a herb;
4. leg - not an organ of the body; 5. dog - not a primate; 6. meadow - not a group of trees; 7. path - not part of a roof; 8. swimming - not played with a ball

Change a Letter :

1. donkey; 2. valley; 3. jockey; 4. Sidney; 5. Paisley; 6. honey; 7. Mersey; 8. Hockney

Islands Around Britain : 1. Anglesey; 2. Guernsey; 3. Orkneys

27c. -a

Odd One Out :

1. aroma - not an animal; 2. Africa - not a country; 3. villa - not a musical instrument; 4. China - not in South America; 5. tarantula - not a snake; 6. tuna - not a fruit; 7. Kenya - not a girl's name; 8. tombola - not to do with music; 9. Canada - not a capital city

Countries and Capitals:

1. Canada - Ottawa; 2. Sri Lanka - Colombo; 3. Venezuela - Caracus;
4. Argentina - Buenos Aires; 5. China - Beijing; 6. Libya - Tripoli;
7. Nicaragua - Managua; 8. Kenya - Nairobi; 9. Cuba - Havana; 10. Ghana - Accra

28c. -i (ē)

Some General Knowledge Questions

1. Florida; 2. India; 3. dog; 4. Japan; 5. Finland; 6. Pacific; 7. New Zealand; 8. female

Food From Around The World

1. chilli con carne - Mexico; 2. chapati - India; 3. muesli - Switzerland; 4. sushi - Japan;
5. Spaghetti - Italy

A Long Name for a Long River: Mississippi

Anagrams : 1. SPAGHETTI; 2. BROCCOLI; 3. SAFARI; 4. CONFETTI;
5. POT-POURRI; 6. GRAFFITI

Mixed Bag Answers

29c. -o (o̅)

Countries, Capital Cities and Continents:
1. Norway/ Oslo/ Europe; 2. Egypt/ Cairo/ Africa; 3. Japan/ Tokyo/ Asia;
4. Sri Lanka/ Colombo/ Asia; 5. Ecuador/ Quito/ South America

Odd One Out : 1. vertigo - not a food; 2. mango - not a musical instrument;
3. cargo - not a living creature; 4. torso - not to do with music

What do these words have in common? : the number three

Synonyms:
cargo/ freight; inferno/ blaze; unaccompanied/ solo; nought/ zero; disguised/ incognito;
buffalo/ bison; hero/ champion; motto/ slogan; keepsake/ memento; gusto/ enthusiasm

30c. -e̅, -i̅ and -u̅

Words Within Words:
1. m<u>e</u>nu; 2. impro<u>mptu</u>; 3. epito<u>me</u>; 4. <u>cat</u>astrophe; 5. anem<u>one</u>; 6. si<u>mile</u>; 7. ap<u>ost</u>rophe

Plurals : 1. fungi; 2. stimuli; 3. cacti; 4. nuclei; 5. thesauri

Synonyms : catastrophe/ disaster; recipe/ formula; teacher/ guru; epitome/ essence;
comparison/ simile; alibi/ excuse; spontaneous/ impromptu

31c. -tial

Anagrams:
1. ESSENTIAL; 2. INITIAL; 3. PARTIAL; 4. CONFIDENTIAL; 5. SPATIAL;
6. CREDENTIALS; 7. TORRENTIAL; 8. RESIDENTIAL; 9. SUBSTANTIAL;
10. POTENTIAL; 11. PREFERENTIAL

Nouns, Verbs and Adjectives
1. confidence/ confide/ confidential; 2. preference/ prefer/ preferential;
3. sequence/ sequence/ sequential; 4. influence/ influence/ influential;
5. residence/ reside/ residential

Missing Words :
1. confidential; 2. impartial; 3. palatial; 4. preferential; 5. substantial; 6. partial

32c. -cial

Find the Mystery Word : 1. facial; 2. artificial; 3. multiracial; 4. official; 5. social;
6. financial; 7. glacial   Mystery Word: crucial

Nouns and Adjectives
1. face/ facial; 2. glacier/ glacial; 3. speciality/ special; 4. race/ racial;
5. benefit/ beneficial; 6. sacrifice/ sacrificial; 7. finance/ financial; 8. province/ provincial

Anagrams : 1. SPECIAL; 2. BENEFICIAL; 3. FINANCIAL; 4. PROVINCIAL

33c. -eon

Something Fishy's Going On Here! :
1. surgeon; 2. truncheon; 3. luncheon; 4. burgeon; 5. bludgeon; 6. chameleon;
7. dungeon; 8. neon

Definitions :
1. burgeon - to flourish or grow rapidly
2. curmudgeon - a bad-tempered person
3. escutcheon - a shield bearing a coat of arms; an ornamental plate round a keyhole

Anagrams: 1. GALLEON; 2. BLUDGEON; 3. DUNGEON; 4. CHAMELEON; 5. PIGEON;
6. SURGEON

Idioms
1. put the cat among the pigeons - to cause trouble
2. something is your pigeon - you have to deal with a situation

Mixed Bag Answers

34c. -gue

Synonyms

plague/ disease; dialogue/ conversation; fatigue/ tiredness; vague/ indistinct; intrigue/ plot; vogue/ fashion; rogue/ cheat; colleague/ workmate; catalogue/ list; prologue/ introduction; brogue/ accent; epilogue/ postscript

Find the Mystery Word

1. colleague; 2. dialogue; 3. fatigue; 4. vague; 5. prologue; 6. synagogue; 7. intrigue;
8. brogue; 9. plague   Mystery Word: catalogue

35c. -ette

Words Within Words

1. baguette; 2. launderette; 3. gazette; 4. maisonette; 5. palette; 6. pipette; 7. rosette;
8. marionette; 9. courgette; 10. layette; 11. cassette; 12. omelette

Definitions: gazette - a newspaper

suffragette - a woman who campaigned for women to have the right to vote

roulette - a gambling game

leatherette - imitation leather

usherette - a woman who shows people to seats in a cinema or theatre

etiquette - the rules of correct social behaviour

36c. -eur

Definitions

coiffeur - a hairdresser

raconteur - a teller of anecdotes

Syllables:

con/ nois/ seur; chauf/ feur; sab/ o/ teur; gran/ deur; am/ a/ teur; sec/ a/ teurs

A Cut Above the Rest:

1. connoisseur; 2. liqueur; 3. chauffeur; 4. saboteur; 5. amateur; 6. entrepreneur;
7. coiffeur; 8. grandeur; 9. masseur

37c. -cian

What's My Line? : 1. musician; 2. optician; 3. electrician

The Experts:

music - musician; mathematics - mathematician; magic - magician; electrics - electrician;
paediatrics - paediatrician; politics - politician